PLAYS IN ACTION
A six-term course in drama

DEREK SLATER

English Lecturer and Drama Specialist,
City of Sheffield Training College

1966
THE QUEEN'S AWARD
TO INDUSTRY 1966

PERGAMON PRESS
OXFORD · LONDON · EDINBURGH · NEW YORK
TORONTO · SYDNEY · PARIS · BRAUNSCHWEIG

Pergamon Press Ltd., Headington Hill Hall, Oxford
4 & 5 Fitzroy Square, London W.1
Pergamon Press (Scotland) Ltd., 2 & 3 Teviot Place, Edinburgh 1
Pergamon Press Inc., 44–01 21st Street, Long Island City, New York 11101
Pergamon of Canada Ltd., 207 Queen's Quay West, Toronto 1
Pergamon Press (Aust.) Pty. Ltd., Rushcutters Bay,
Sydney, New South Wales
Pergamon Press S.A.R.L., 24 rue des Écoles, Paris 5ᵉ
Vieweg & Sohn GmbH, Burgplatz 1, Braunschweig

Copyright © 1964 Pergamon Press Ltd.

First edition 1964

Reprinted 1968

Library of Congress Catalog Card No. 64–8775

Printed in Great Britain by A. Wheaton & Co., Exeter and London

08 101992 0 (flexicover)
08 201992 4 (hard cover)
08 301992 8 (flexicover non-net)

Contents

Acknowledgements

THE author wishes to express his grateful thanks for permission to quote from copyright material:

To Samuel French Limited, for permission to quote from *Fool's Errand* by Margaret Wood, and *Sunday Costs Five Pesos* by Josephina Niggli.

To Messrs. Heinemann for permission to quote from *Noah* by André Obey, and *An Enemy of the People* by Henrik Ibsen.

To Grove Publications Inc. for permission to quote from *The Caucasian Chalk Circle* by Bertolt Brecht.

To the Incorporated Society of Authors for permission to quote from *The Devil's Disciple* by Bernard Shaw.

To A. M. Heath & Company for permission to quote from *The Insect Play* by Karel and Josef Čapek.

To Curtis Brown Limited for permission to quote from *Richard of Bordeaux* by Gordon Daviot.

Introduction

THIS is not a textbook for the specialist who is more interested in stagecraft than anything else; nor is it primarily intended for the student whose preoccupation with plays is exclusively literary, and who is pursuing their study merely for examination purposes. It attempts to steer a middle course: that is to say, to encourage teacher and pupil to enjoy drama by reading it, reading about it, and acting it. It is based on the conviction that the best way to appreciate a play is to be aware of its effect in performance.

The book is divided into two parts. The first—and shorter—section is intended as a general introduction to the whole field of drama. It raises questions which are relevant not only to performances in the professional theatre, but to the enjoyment of play reading, cinema, and television drama. It attempts to deal with the relationship between the text and the performance, and it is recommended that these three chapters, read by the teacher with the class, might provide the basis for fruitful discussion, and also prepare for the second—and major—section of the book.

The second part of the book is a closer study of individual plays. The basis on which these have been selected is made clear in the preface to Part II of the book, and it should be emphasised that, in order to derive the maximum benefit from this section, the class should be prepared to study the complete texts of all the plays discussed. While certain passages have been quoted as illustration, and certain scenes selected as particularly suitable for dramatisation by the class, it is obviously unreasonable to expect the pupils to appreciate the full impact of the play unless they have had the opportunity of reading it in its complete form.

To make this kind of study possible, it should be mentioned that many of the plays are available in cheap editions. The two

Shakespeare plays should present no problem for most schools; all the one-act plays are obtainable in acting editions from Samuel French and Co.; the plays by Brecht, Synge, Daviot and Shaw are available in paperbacks. In the case of the Ibsen I have used the William Archer translation, and the text of *And So Ad Infinitym* (as I point out below) is the acting version prepared by Nigel Playfair from the original—and only—translation.

PART ONE

WHAT MAKES A PLAY?

"Now unity, however desirable in political agitations, is fatal to drama; for every drama must present a conflict. The end may be reconciliation or destruction; or, as in life itself, there may be no end; but the conflict is indispensable: no conflict, no drama."

SHAW: Preface to *Plays Pleasant*

Preface to Part One

THE three chapters which follow attempt to deal with three related questions:

1. What do we mean by *drama*?
2. What are the problems of plays *in performance*?
3. Can we understand the plays better by trying parts of them out for ourselves?

1. Introduction

What do we mean by "Drama"?

One way to answer this question would be to pick up a diction-ary; or, perhaps, to turn to a reference library to see what Drama meant to the Greeks, or the Romans, or the people of Elizabethan England. But a simpler and a more sensible way would be to pick up a daily newspaper. There the word "drama" is always turning up, in headlines like SEA RESCUE DRAMA, or SOLDIER'S DRAMATIC ESCAPE, or COURTROOM DRAMA SENSATION. If we ask ourselves what kinds of stories these headlines represent, we may save ourselves a trip to the dictionary or the reference library.

The one common factor in all these stories is *excitement*. In all of them there is something to make us hold our breath. Will the crew of the wrecked ship be saved? Will the prisoner manage to escape? Will the accused man be found guilty? In other words, there is always some feeling of suspense to arouse our interest in the story. And that means that there is always some kind of *struggle*—the old writers used the word "conflict", which means much the same thing—till the matter is finally settled, one way or the other.

So we can say, to begin with, that a good play is about a struggle of some kind. But we have to realise that just any kind of struggle will not do. A fifteen-round heavyweight contest may be very exciting, but it would not make a very good play. A cup final may be very dramatic, but there is nothing very remarkable about Tottenham Hotspur taking on a village football team and beating them 25–0. To keep us interested, the contest has to be a pretty even one, so that the result is not obvious before it begins; and, before we can put the contest on to the stage, it has to be about something more than just physical strength, or sporting

5

skill. A fight may be an important event in a play, but it is not the *whole* play.

Remember, too, that not all successful plays have as much violent action as a boxing match or a game of football. The most popular television serial may be about very ordinary people, who live in a very ordinary street, and whose lives are not full of gay adventure; but there is plenty of argument, plenty of suspense, there are constant little rows and squabbles, caused by jealousy, or envy, or selfishness—in fact, we recognise these same faults in our own neighbours, and in ourselves. Many plays, more exciting and more important than a television serial, deal with distinguished or famous people, people who hold positions of trust in government, or in the Church, or in their own town or city, and whose problems are therefore bigger, more serious, and more difficult to solve. There is still a struggle of some kind; and the sight of a character trying to overcome his business rivals, or fighting to prove his innocence in a corrupt court, or being forced to choose between staying with a wife he no longer cares for and abandoning his family to begin a new life abroad— these can be more exciting than a boxing match or a game of football.

We are all interested in the way other people behave, but we become very much more interested when we learn what kind of people they are. Before we can really settle down to enjoy the conflicts in a good play, we have to be able to form some opinion of the characters involved; and so the playwright has to show us, in one way or another, what kind of people he is writing about. He wants us to be interested in what they are doing, and so he has to make them into interesting people first.

This business of "character" is very important. You might say that many a play is little more than a story, with the events acted instead of described. But in a good story not everything happens by accident; somebody in the story has to make things happen, and this is true whether the story is written as a novel, or acted as a play upon a stage. Suppose that, at the opening of a play, a rich man is quarrelling with his wife because she is extravagant. He may be a miser, who can easily afford to pay his wife's bills; he may be a generous and sensible man, who wants to cure her of her wasteful spending; or he may be a proud man, pretending to be richer than he really is, but in fact in danger of being ruined if she doesn't stop. What happens in Acts II and III really depends, among other things, on what kind of man he is.

So a playwright makes a play about interesting people, and what happens when their lives become tangled up with each other, or with a problem caused by the world in which they live. Sometimes his play ends tragically, because the hero or heroine is overcome, and loses the fight; sometimes the play ends happily, because the characters triumph over their difficulties.

A play with a "happy ending" is usually called a comedy; but when we hear the word "comedy" we usually think of something amusing, and it is often true that a play which takes a light-hearted view of life, which never for a moment looks as if it is going to be serious, has the effect of making us laugh. But what is it, exactly, that we laugh at?

In quite a lot of comedy, we are really laughing at ourselves. The playwright puts people on the stage with familiar human faults or weaknesses, and the action of the play shows up these weaknesses until they become comic. The boaster is made to look foolish; the miser is made to hand over his money; the snobbish woman is "brought down a peg"—and so on. We laugh; yet we all have our moments of bragging, or selfishness, or pride, just as the people in the play have.

Sometimes—and this is specially true of farce—the playwright takes a short cut, and gives us comic characters which we recognise because we have grown familiar with them. In plays of this type, all professors are absent-minded, all clergymen are half-wits, all mothers-in-law are dragons, all spinsters are humourless, all children are monsters, and all men over the age of forty are not to be trusted. Having created these absurd characters, the playwright proceeds to invent a series of coincidences which will make the absurdity seem all the worse. In these plays, terrible things happen to the characters, but nobody minds, for nobody would ever dream of taking them seriously.

Sometimes, whether in comedy or not, we laugh at a character because he says amusing things. If he is really part of the play, the amusing things he is saying will have something to do with what the play is about: he may be making fun of another person, or commenting on the foolish behaviour of someone in the play. In this case, while we may laugh at what he is saying, we may not find the whole play amusing at all—in fact, the remarks of this one person may help us to see how serious the whole thing really is.

Some plays are serious, some not; but there is no clear line between comedy and tragedy, and we must not be surprised to find that there are things to laugh at in the most serious plays, and gay comedies with quite a serious idea behind them.

"*The two-hour traffic of the stage*"

One of the things which makes plays different from novels, films, and poems, is the question of *size*. A play can only last two to three hours, and in that short time the whole story has to be told. What is more, it cannot really have an enormous number of characters—they wouldn't fit on to the stage, and in any case no theatre management could afford to employ so many. This means that the playwright has to concentrate on one small part of the story—the part which is really the most exciting aspect. He also has to arrange things so that only the really important people in the story are brought into it. If the story he wants to tell is complicated, then he has to make sure that, as the play goes along, the audience can pick up information about previous happenings from what the characters say. If the story is spread over many years, then the play has to skip over the unimportant bits, and show us just the ones that matter.

Let me give you some examples. T. S. Eliot's play *Murder in the Cathedral* is about Thomas à Becket. During the first act we learn a great deal about the early life of the archbishop, but the actual play begins less than a week before his death, and concentrates on the events of his last hours. In Marlowe's *Dr. Faustus* a period of twenty-four years is covered by the play, but when the play opens Faustus is already an ageing scholar. In Act I he sells his soul to the devil; in Act V he dies horribly; in between we see a little of the way he spent his twenty-four years, but we are really more interested in how he will behave when his time is up.

Having to concentrate our attention in this way is a decided advantage. It makes the "conflict" in the play all the more intense, and there is less chance that our attention will wander. It also means that some things have to be left to our imagination, and that helps to increase our enjoyment. For, if our imaginations are stimulated, our pleasure is all the greater.

Why is "using your imagination" so important? Well, the truth is that nobody can enjoy a play—or a film, or TV programme—without having to pretend a little. Perhaps there is a famous actor pretending to be Napoleon and we pretend to believe him. If the film is exciting, we forget the cameras, although we know they must be there. Little children turn a table upside down, and pretend that it's a ship: or they turn the garage into a cave, or the attic into a prison cell, and they play happily for hours. The theatre is just like that: the author asks us to play the game with him, and if the story is exciting enough, we do.

Plain or fancy dress?

If you look at a history of costume, you will notice how very often people in the past changed the style of the clothes they wore, just as they changed the style of their houses, and their way of speaking. The history of the theatre has been rather like this. The Greeks played in huge open-air theatres, their actors wearing masks, and the performance being accompanied by dancing, singing, and—sometimes—clowning; in Shakespeare's time people went "to hear a play"—they cared little for scenery (there wasn't any), or costume (the actors wore their own clothes), or glamour (the women's parts were played by men or boys); the words were enough for them.

In every age the theatre has offered its audiences something different. A tragedy first performed in 1610 or thereabouts ended with the stage littered with corpses; just over a century later, most of the audience walked out in disgust because there was *one* murder on the stage. Our ancestors, the Victorians, filled their stages with costly and elaborate scenery, complicated lighting, and rich costumes, and it would be difficult to revive some of their plays without great trouble and expense. On the other hand, they took exactly the same trouble with Shakespeare, and yet many of us have seen Shakespeare performed in the open air, or in modern dress, or with no scenery at all.

Is it possible, do you think, that a good play, a really good play, does not depend for its success upon expensive staging? This is probably true; but it does need actors who understand the characters, a producer who can help them to play the scenes effectively, and a way of staging which will give the play the right atmosphere—or, in other words, will help the audience to "pretend".

Living in the twentieth century, we are extremely fortunate. We can look back at the different ways in which plays were performed, and we can choose the way which suits us. Or, better still, we can build theatres which can be easily adapted for different kinds of performance. Most of our best theatres are quite small, so that the actors are never very far from their audiences; and most of our theatres have up-to-date equipment —especially lighting—so that we can achieve interesting and varied stage effects without the difficulties and expense which this used to cause.

The main thing to remember is that all the skill in the world, of acting, production, costume, scenery and so on, cannot turn a bad play into a good one. That is why, in most modern theatres, plays are presented as simply as possible, so that we can enjoy watching the characters without having to worry whether the effects will succeed or fail. Some theatres have been built in which the audience sit on all four sides of the stage, so close that they really feel to be part of the performance; obviously, in this kind of theatre, where built-up scenery cannot be used, the excitement comes from the *acting*, and from nothing else. And if what the actors are saying and doing is dull, or unreal, or confusing, then we are not going to enjoy the play at all.

Illusion and reality

You can probably understand from what I have been saying that, in spite of the many different ways there are of putting a play on the stage, the most important part of it is the text—the words written by the playwright and spoken by the actors. But, just as there have been many ways of *staging* plays, so there have been many ways of *writing* them—and it is quite likely that somebody is inventing a new way at this very moment. You must have noticed that the heroes of Shakespeare's plays are almost always kings, or noblemen, or great warriors, or famous figures from history; and that they speak in a way quite different from that of ordinary people. We never see them sitting in the quiet of their own homes, performing some simple domestic duty; they are always engaged on some world-shaking enterprise, or involved in some tremendously important decision. They are quite remote from the ordinary life of ordinary people, and this is why it is stupid to put these plays on the stage as if they were "slices of life". A Shakespeare play has many scenes, following swiftly one after the other, and it would ruin the play if we held up the action by trying to build realistic scenery. Besides, the words tell us where we are and what we are doing, and the play moves so quickly that we are carried along by the powerful language and the excitement of the plot.

Turn from Shakespeare to a modern play. Here there is probably only one scene, and—since the hero is a bank clerk—it is certainly not a royal palace. Perhaps, during the course of the first act, he discovers, some time after returning home from the bank, that his wife has grown tired of him, and has decided to leave home. A common occurrence, you might say, since many marriages are not entirely successful, and sometimes one partner or the other decides not to put up with it any longer. But our hero does not immediately realise what has happened, and he may have to deal with the grocer's boy, and the nosey woman next door, and a couple of telephone calls. He is probably a bit hungry or thirsty, and so he makes himself a sandwich, or pours himself a drink. And, when he talks, he does not talk in blank verse, but in something like the language of ordinary people. What is more—unlike the hero in a Shakespeare play—he never talks to himself, because this is something which most ordinary people do not do.

The differences between these two plays are obvious. But is one more "real" than the other? No, not necessarily. Admittedly the Shakespeare play does not try to copy the lives of ordinary people, but that does not mean that the characters are not just as convincing. The noble hero has feelings of greed, jealousy, hatred and ambition, just like the man next door. He may speak in complicated poetry, instead of the way most of us speak; but that is only because he is expressing the **kind** of feelings we all have but cannot always put into words. Our bank clerk has to bother about callers, and telephone messages, and letters, and cups of tea, and grocery bills, because these are all an important part of his life; things like this are left out of the Shakespeare play in order to make room for more important things.

In a good play—a really good play—*everything* is important. Even in plays about bank clerks, the most ordinary happenings are used to tell us what kind of people the characters are, who their friends are, what kinds of lives they lead. A modern "realistic" play, as we call it, is no more realistic than the plays of the past. Its characters may be more ordinary, but they are not necessarily more true to life.

What seems to matter—whether it is Shakespeare or not—is that the characters should appear to think and act like recognisable human beings. If this is so, we can then sympathise with some of them, dislike others, and take a real interest in how their lives turn out. But there is a kind of play whose characters are not quite like this. They still resemble human beings, but this time they are exaggerated, usually to make us laugh, or to make fun of the kind of people they represent. We call such characters "types"—some of them are modern, some not, but they all have the kind of weaknesses that we recognise. Sometimes their names give them away: LYDIA LANGUISH, a foolishly romantic girl; SIR TUNBELLY CLUMSY, a loud and domineering country squire; TRIBULATION WHOLESOME, a comical clergyman. Sometimes they do not even have names: MR A. and MRS. A. are the typical husband and wife in a play written in 1935, and their daily lives are supposed to be the same as thousands of others; and, in a famous German play of the 1920s, the author goes even further, calling his characters simply THE MOTHER; THE BOSS; THE WORKER; and so on.

So you see, fashions in writing plays, like fashions in performing them, are constantly changing. At the moment, in 1964, the fashion is for plays about the personal problems of ordinary people, but that does not mean that all plays being written nowadays are like this; many theatres are experimenting with plays of all kinds, just as they are trying out new productions of plays from previous generations. The plays studied in this book are of many kinds, and from several countries. In fact, although there are two plays by Shakespeare, there are not two plays alike, in style or subject-matter, and yet nearly all of them were written within the last hundred years. They have been chosen because of their variety, for in this way you will learn more about what the theatre has to offer; but they have also been chosen because they are good plays of their kind, and therefore you should get a lot of excitement out of reading them, and trying out some of the scenes for yourselves.

2. Plays in Performance

As you study the plays suggested in this book, you should always bear in mind that they were written to be acted. Even a poor performance of a good play (and no performance could ever be perfect) gives more of the flavour of the thing than merely reading it. There are various reasons for this. If the characters are interesting, it is easier to become excited about them if they are represented by actual human beings; that is why, in many cases, a stage play is more gripping than a film, though it may not be as good. Another reason is that the point of a scene, or at least a part of it, may be a visual one—that is to say, it may depend on something the acter is *seen* to do (such as hiding something, or stealing some small but important object, and so on), or it may be expressed in *action* rather than words. This may be violent action, or it may not. The crucial scene may contain a duel (as in *Hamlet*), a murder, or a suicide; or it may be something quite subtle but no less important (a forgiving handshake between two men who have been bitter enemies, or the payment of a debt). It is true to say that the final moments of quite a number of plays are wordless, and it is also true to say that many of the other "big moments" in these plays depend upon action to some degree or other.

It is, of course, quite possible for an imaginative reader to picture the whole scene in his mind, without the help of actors at all. But if you take part in any kind of play, you soon realise that it is not merely the behaviour of the main actors which is important. Suppose that, in a play, a visitor calls on a husband and wife to tell the husband that his brother has been killed in a rail accident. The caller speaks to the husband, who is—naturally—very upset; but his wife's expression, her manner, the way she speaks her next line may tell us a great deal. Perhaps she is secretly rather pleased at the news, and is at the same time careful not to let her husband notice the fact. This is something she can show to the audience, but it is not something which is easily imagined in reading the play. Take a more famous example: after the murder of Julius Caesar, first Brutus, then Antony, speaks to the crowd. Brutus is popular, and the crowd are so much behind him that they are reluctant to give Antony a hearing at all; but gradually, as he speaks, they are completely won over to his point of view. The most important actor in that scene is not the man who speaks Antony's words, nor the man who plays Brutus. The scene depends on the reactions of a group of "citizens" who show, by their behaviour, what effect the main speakers are having on the crowd of Romans.

The people who say that a good play is better read than acted are really afraid that, by a bad production or performance, the play will suffer. They would rather not run the risk of bad acting and production spoiling a play of which they have become very fond. We must sympathise with them a little. After all, no musician likes to hear his favourite piece of music played at the wrong speed, or with handfuls of wrong notes. But the rest of us, who are not musicians, would rather hear it along with a few mistakes than miss the pleasure of hearing it at all. A good play is rather like music, to this extent: that it is better to have a performance than merely to sit and look at it on the printed page.

No two performances of the same play are ever really alike. Not only do different actors see the characters differently, but also different producers have different ideas about what the play means. Of course, this does not mean that most plays are so peculiar that the meaning is anybody's guess; but it does mean that different productions can show up different aspects—or, in other words, different productions may emphasise different things. Perhaps, if we take a closer look at one play, you will see what I mean.

Three ways of doing it

Some years ago, J. B. Priestley wrote a play called *An Inspector Calls*. Here is the story.

In a Yorkshire industrial town a small party is in progress. Father is a prosperous manufacturer, and his daughter is becoming engaged to marry a go-ahead young man. This should be a good match, for the father not only has hopes of a title; he also hopes that his new son-in-law will bring valuable business contacts with him. There is another person present— a son, the fiancée's younger brother.

Suddenly, the party is interrupted by the arrival of a police officer in plain clothes, calling himself Inspector Goole. A young woman has been admitted to the local hospital, having poisoned herself by drinking a bottle of disinfectant, and the inspector is asking a few questions. He has with him a photograph of the girl, which he shows to each member of the family in turn; and, as he does so, each one recognises the girl. It seems that each one of them, in some way, has contributed to the girl's misery. Father sacked her from his firm because she was active in a strike for better wages; and since losing that job, she has come into contact with all of them—including Gerald, the prospective son-in-law—and each time with unfortunate results.

Having successfully blighted the pleasure of their evening, the inspector leaves. But now comes the strange thing. Gerald and the daughter have quarrelled, largely as a result of the inspector's visit, and Gerald has left the house. He returns, with the news that no such person as Inspector Goole is known to the local police. A quick telephone call soon establishes that no girl has been brought into hospital as a suicide case. What then? Have they imagined the whole thing? Was the strange inspector a supernatural figure, a kind of Voice of Conscience? Did he, as Gerald suggests, produce five *different* photographs, one for each of them, and make them believe that they were the same person?

At this point, a split occurs within the group. Mother, father, and Gerald take the selfish view that "everything is all right" and that they need not worry any more; son and daughter, having more tender consciences, point out that, whoever the inspector was, it does not make them less guilty. The argument is interrupted by a ring of the telephone. The voice at the other end informs them that a young woman has just been admitted to hospital, having drunk a bottle of disinfectant, and that "an inspector is on his way round to ask them a few questions".

The action of this interesting play is continuous, and takes place in one room. When the play was first produced in England, every care was taken to make it as realistic as possible. The actors spoke with Yorkshire accents, and the stage setting was a careful reproduction of a middle-class house in the north of England. Every detail of furniture—expensive, but slightly showy—was studied to give just the right impression of this family. When the curtain rose on Act II, the room appeared to have been turned round slightly, so that a little more of one side, and a little less of the other, was now visible; and the same thing happened at the beginning of Act III. By the time the play was over, the audience had seen most of the room, and could easily believe that the actors were impersonating real and ordinary people.

When the play was produced in Russia, things were very different. No attempt was made to build a "real" room on the stage. Instead, the actors performed on a huge circular platform, open to the skies, with a high ceiling but no walls; the stars of the night sky could be seen twinkling in a deep blue setting; the furniture and costumes were simple and timeless. The only unusual feature was a huge door, standing at the back of the stage. In other words, whoever designed this production was not interested in Yorkshire, or the little lives of ordinary people, and so the production stressed the *symbolic* side of the play. The action could be anywhere, at any time, and the idea was that people the world over—rich or poor, Yorkshire or Russian—have the same sort of problems on their consciences. Whereas the London production wanted the audience to recognise the place and the people, the Russian production underplayed the realistic part of the play, and emphasised instead the mysterious inspector in his role of judge.

Finally, not many years ago, a film was made of this same play. Films get many of their best effects by the use of the camera to make the situation more dramatic, and so the story, as we might expect, was not content to remain in one room. As the inspector continued his questioning, we were *shown* the girl, first with one character, then another, as each one became involved in her life. This was no doubt very interesting to the cinema audiences, especially those who had never seen the play; but it almost completely destroyed the "mystery" of who the inspector was, and whether in fact there was one girl, or several. That is to say, by showing us everything that was *supposed* to have happened, we were never allowed the pleasure of wondering whether it really happened or not.

From this short look at the fortunes of just one play, perhaps you can see why performances can always teach us something new and important, which we could not hope to get from reading alone; and perhaps you can also see why (as we said in the previous chapter of this book) a good play will always leave a good deal to the imagination of the audience.

Telling the audience the truth

Before you go on to study the plays discussed in this book, it might be useful to see where we have got to. We have formed some impression of what makes a play—or, in other words, we know what to expect from the plays in this book; and we have agreed, I hope, that costume, scenery, and details of stage presentation, however important they may be, cannot turn a bad play into a good one, although they *can* help to make a play more effective when it is performed. We have also reached the conclusion that a play needs to be performed because, while it is true that performances can harm or misrepresent a play, they can also throw new light on it, or show us things about it which we had not previously realised. I hope, therefore, that as you read and study the plays suggested here, you will also perform parts of them—not, of course, with a view to giving a public performance, but as a way of getting to know the characters, and finding out what means the playwright has used to make his drama effective.

Some of the people who write plays have very definite ideas about how their plays should be performed, and many playwrights of the past were writing for theatres which no longer exist. In introducing plays of different types, I have tried to describe the kind of theatre for which they were intended, and to suggest the kind of performance which the play asks for; but these suggestions do not sweep away all the difficulties. It is obviously impossible, for example, to perform Shakespeare as he was performed 400 years ago, although there are one or two eccentrics who say that this is the only fair way to do it. It is equally stupid (or it seems so to us) to perform him in ornate modern costume and extravagant scenery, as was done in the eighteenth century, so that the actor playing King Lear or Julius Caesar strutted about the stage in a silk waistcoat and knee breeches, and with silver buckles to his shoes. The argument in favour of this absurdity is as follows: "Shakespearean actors wore their own, everyday clothes; why should not our eighteenth-century actors do the same?". Put the question in modern terms, and you will immediately see the answer. You see, while the average member of the audience is not at all sure what the royal family of Ancient Britain wore when out visiting, he is quite certain that they did *not* wear dark lounge suits and carry rolled umbrellas.

Some time after Charles Laughton made the famous film *The Private Life of Henry VIII* he received a letter complaining that the nightdresses worn in the bedchamber scene (between Henry and Anne of Cleves) were not historically accurate. Mr Laughton replied that he was aware of this, but pointed out that, in that particular period, it was the custom of the English to go to bed without clothes of any kind. The search for absolute historical accuracy is liable to lead to that sort of difficulty. But this rather frivolous example does illustrate a serious question: if we cannot perform plays as they were performed in the author's own time, and we cannot simply transfer them to our own stages, what is the best thing to do?

The answer is not, after all, very complicated. By reading the play, we can usually form a reasonable idea of what the playwright is trying to say, and we can then put his play on to the stage in such a way that a modern audience will accept and understand it. We do not build an Elizabethan theatre; but we recognise, as we read a play like *Macbeth*, that the production should allow for violent action, and swift-moving scenes— following each other in quick succession, (especially in the last act) to give the impression of the forces of justice advancing upon the tyrant. If we read a little more carefully, we notice how often the play mentions darkness and gloom, and how much superstition there is; and so we realise that it is more important to create the right atmosphere than to worry about getting the right pattern in the Scottish soldiers' kilts. A brief glance at some of the great, roaring speeches tells us that this is no play for actors who are afraid of opening their mouths, for all the characters in this play give full and noisy expression to their feelings. You can, of course, see why: for in Shakespeare's time, without the help of costume, lighting, and stage effects, it must have been the powerful speech which carried the play along.

Sometimes the playwright himself gives a clear indication of how his play should be performed, but that does not mean that he is always, necessarily, right. Bernard Shaw mistrusted both audiences and producers, and so, whenever his play is set in modern times, he gives extremely detailed instructions about the set, down to the last chair, picture, or ornament. When it comes to the characters he goes even further, describing not merely the kind of people they are, but also their dress, age, personal appearance, and mannerisms. This is very useful, and very helpful, because it gives a clear indication of what Shaw had in mind; but it is quite unnecessary (even if it were possible) to insist that the hero should be ". . . of middling stature, and undistinguished appearance, with strong neck and shoulders, roundish obstinate-looking head covered with short crisp bronze curls . . ." and so on. But Shaw himself abandoned the suffocating detail of his Victorian and Edwardian plays when the subject was not a contemporary one. He does not attempt a detailed description of the Italian inn in which Napoleon spent part of the summer of 1796; and he knew enough about the theatre to know that no management could reproduce realistically the seven elaborate scenes of *St. Joan*. Somehow the spirit of medieval France must be captured on the stage, but it does not need the services of an architect to do it.

At the other end of the scale, there are playwrights who have definite theories about how a play should be presented, and who write their intentions into their plays. They were deliberately trying to break away from the usual style of thing, and their wishes should as far as possible be respected. Thornton Wilder, for example, for reasons which are discussed later, wanted his actors, without the help of furniture or hand-properties, to suggest the actions of the characters by mime, and it would be quite wrong for them to perform otherwise. Obey was writing for an experimental theatre which believed in the importance of movement on the stage, and this is very obvious as soon as you read one of his plays. Brecht had his own special theory about the way the actors should present the characters in his "epic dramas". The simplicity of these three dramatists is in sharp contrast with the detail demanded by Shaw and others.

Somewhere in between comes the playwright who writes for the theatre he knows, and leaves it to the actors and producer to put his play across. He has no axe to grind; he is neither fastidious nor revolutionary; he has been to the theatre, he knows what kind of things are done there, and he writes a play which he hopes will be performed with success. If he is a modern play-wright, and he wants to make money, his play probably has one setting, and a small cast, and we have no difficulty in deciding how it should be performed. If he is ancient Greek, or Elizabethan, he gives us the bare text, with no stage directions, and the choice of method of production is left entirely to us.

3. Characters and Situations

ONE of the best ways of finding out something of the art of the playwright is to act out parts of his play. To do this properly would require the learning of lines, and there is not always time for this, and even a play-reading of the scene needs to be rehearsed, for nobody could possibly understand the characters at the first glance. So many so-called "drama lessons" in schools turn out to be no more than rather disappointing play readings; and yet the same pupils, after several months of careful preparation, are capable of giving a very successful public performance of a play. If we are going to look at two full-length plays every term we certainly have no time to prepare a public performance, but there is no reason why we should not do something more than merely reading the play in the classroom.

Improvisation

Actors have not always used scripts. In Medieval times, when church services were conducted in Latin, it became the practice to perform certain parts of the bible story so that the large majority of the congregation could understand and enjoy them. Although these plays came later to be written down, it is true to say that for a long time the lines were invented by the actors each time the play was given. The actors were told which character they were supposed to represent, and what the scene was about, and they then proceeded to "improvise" the play. To lay aside the script, and persuade actors to imagine the situation and make up the lines is still an excellent way of getting them to realise what kind of persons they are supposed to be. In fact, as recently as 1940, in a film called *The Magnificent Ambersons*, the director, Orson Welles, filmed the whole of one long scene using the words made up by the actors, there and then, in front of the cameras. The scene was a great success.

There are a number of ways in which we can improvise short scenes for ourselves. Here are some of them:

(1) We can improvise scenes *in our own characters*. Imagine that you have met a friend whom you have not seen for a couple of years; visit a house where a friend is recovering from an illness; start an argument, with two or three other people, about how you are going to spend your weekend; or turn the whole class into a meeting to decide how the school should spend a large sum of money which has been unexpectedly given to it.

There are hundreds of similar situations which you can think of, but in each one you are playing the part of yourself, instead of pretending to be somebody else.

(2) We can improvise scenes *with different characters*. You are a bad-tempered customer, going back to a department store to complain about something you have bought; a number of you are guests (relations, family friends) at a wedding party; or refugees, anxiously waiting for news from the customs or the immigration authorities; or the whole classroom becomes a hospital ward, with patients, nurses, doctors, visitors, and so on.

Again, the choice is unlimited. But this time, before you can begin, you have to decide who you are, and what kind of person. Then, as the scene develops, your character and situation will be revealed by the things you say and do.

(3) We can improvise scenes *based on the play we are reading*. Here, before progressing beyond the actual story, we can imagine ourselves acting certain parts of it, and then, perhaps, comparing the scene as we invented it with the author's much more professional version.

The value of this is to make us realise what the author's problem was. We can try to work out for ourselves what the various people in the play are likely to say and do in the particular situation, and then, when we come to read the actual scene in the play, we discover how the playwright wanted the scene to go. Sometimes we find ourselves disagreeing with him, saying things like "But nobody would have said a thing like that in those circumstances". This criticism is very important, because it is helping us to understand the play.

Scripted scenes

Another way to enjoy drama by doing it, without the necessity of learning pages of dialogue, is to study very closely a short scene—a really short scene, often no more than a few lines long. A very instructive place to begin is the beginning of the play, for it is here that the playwright is revealing his characters and his situation to the audience. Remember that, at the beginning of a play, the audience knows nothing at all, and the writer has to tell them quite a lot, and at the same time make them ask questions, so that they do not lose interest in the plot before it really gets going.

Let us take a look at a short, simple example, taken from *I Have Been Here Before* by Priestley. The curtain rises on a pleasant room in an ordinary English country inn. We have just time to learn that the season is Whitsuntide, and that the landlord and his sister are expecting a busy weekend, when the door opens, and a middle-aged man, who speaks with a German or Austrian accent, enters. The landlord is alone at the time.

DR. GORTLER: Good evening.
LANDLORD: Good evening.
DR. GORTLER: You are the landlord?
LANDLORD: Yes, that's right. Sam Shipley.
DR. GORTLER: You let rooms to visitors?
LANDLORD: Yes.
DR. GORTLER: Three or four perhaps?
LANDLORD: Yes.
                    (at this moment SALLY *enters)*
SALLY: Oh! Good evening.
DR. GORTLER: Good evening.
SALLY: Were you wanting a room?
DR. GORTLER: I am not sure.
SALLY: Oh? Well, it doesn't matter, because I'm afraid we can't oblige you.

It could hardly be more unexciting. What is more (apart from the accent, and that is not really important in this short scene) it is very easy to act. But it is full of interesting things. Who is this stranger? Why does he ask, not about one room, but about several? And then, when he is asked if he wishes to stay there himself, he is "not sure". What, then, does he want?

He interests us, not because of his character, since we know nothing about him yet, but because of his strange attitude. Yet we want to know more about him, and so we continue to listen with interest.

What about the others? There is nothing remarkable about them, surely? No, there isn't; but they are an interesting contrast to each other. Sam, when asked "You are the landlord?" could have simply replied, "Yes". But he announces his name, which makes us think that he is perhaps an easy-going, friendly sort of chap. The rest of his part contains the one word, "Yes". But look back at the script. The first time, he is answering the question about rooms to let; but the second time, wouldn't he sound a little bit surprised? Why does a man, travelling alone, want to know about "three or four" rooms? If Sam doesn't sound surprised, the audience might not notice the odd question. So you see, even the word "Yes" is important here.

And now, what about Sally? Notice that Sam waited for the stranger to ask his questions, whereas Sally says, immediately, "Were you wanting a room?" She is much more brisk and businesslike than her brother, and we can't help noticing how quickly she dismisses the stranger with her last line. An interesting situation: an amiable landlord, his sharp-tongued sister, and a mysterious foreigner, who has obviously come to look for someone, or to meet someone, or . . .? But we must wait a little longer to find out.

You will have noticed that this scrap of dialogue needs no stage directions to tell us how the lines should be spoken, nor do we need to know the rest of the plot. Sometimes, of course, a scene as short as this makes nonsense unless we know the whole story, but that need not stop us from trying it out, when we have read the whole play perhaps. It does not have to be from the beginning of the play, though this is often the best place; it might be a few lines in which something very vital happens—at a *climax* of the action. Here is one such example.

It comes from the second act of Arthur Miller's play *The*

Crucible. The testimony of a number of young girls has caused many innocent women to be accused of witchcraft. One of the girls, Mary Warren, servant to John Proctor and his wife, has returned to Proctor's farm and is describing the court's activities.

MARY WARREN: . . . You must see it, sir, it's God's work we do. So I'll be gone every day for some time. I'm—I'm an official of the court, they say, and I——
PROCTOR: I'll official you!
MARY: I'll not stand whipping any more!
ELIZABETH: Mary, promise now you'll stay at home——
MARY: The Devil's loose in Salem, Mr. Proctor, we must discover where he's hiding!
PROCTOR: I'll whip the Devil out of you!
MARY: I saved *her* life today!
ELIZABETH: I am accused?
MARY: Somewhat mentioned . . .

Here the author's stage directions help us a little, but we can still interpret the scene without them. Proctor grabs his whip on his first line, which prompts Mary to say "I'll not stand whipping any more!" Elizabeth Proctor tries to intervene; but on Proctor's next line (when he actually mentions whipping) the whip is about to fall. Suddenly, as Mary points to Elizabeth in desperation, we can imagine the stunned silence; Proctor lowering his arm; and then the quiet question from his wife—"I am accused?" This is only one of many climaxes in this grim and powerful play.

You will see from this that we do not need stage directions to tell us how the characters move on the stage. We can imagine Mary shrinking away from Proctor, and we can imagine him striding angrily up to her to beat the nonsense out of her silly head. She is both proud of being an "official" and afraid of Proctor's anger. Elizabeth tries, with her first line, to come between them, by appealing to Mary, but it is too late. The damage has been done.

By looking closely at short snatches of dialogues we learn a lot about the actor's job. By looking at longer extracts we can study the play more fully. We can form an impression of the movement, not of one or two characters, but of quite large groups. We can judge whether the scene goes quickly or slowly, and whether it gets its effects by swirling, violent action, or by tension created through pauses, silences, and sudden outbursts. We can also judge the different results when very ordinary language is used (as in these two examples) compared with verse, or long speeches, or the same kind of line repeated many times. The plays which follow, in the second part of this book, contain examples of all kinds of writing for the stage.

Finally, a word of warning. If you decide to try out some of these longer scenes, you may find that a classroom is not always big enough. However, I think it would be a mistake to use a platform stage, even if one happens to be available. Most stages permit the audience to sit to one side only, and this means that, without the aid of a skilled director, the actors are often in each other's way, or "masked", as we say, from those watching. It is probably better if the audience sit all round the group of actors, leaving them a space in the middle to perform the scene; in this way everybody is close enough to see and hear what is happening, to offer comment or criticism. The actors can be natural, because they do not have to raise their voices to be heard, and it takes no time at all for one player to be replaced by someone watching. In Elizabethan times, the audiences crowded round the stage, and some of the wealthier ones perched on stools on the stage itself—and what was good enough for Shakespeare is probably good enough for us.

Part Two
A SIX-TERM COURSE IN DRAMA

> "Every great play we have ever been lucky enough to
> feast our eyes on has come out of a popular playhouse."
>
> WALTER KERR: *How not to write a play*

Preface to Part Two

THE plays selected for study in the second part of this book have been chosen for a number of reasons. They contain, taken as a whole, a great variety of themes and treatments, because one of the most fascinating things about the theatre, particularly in our time, is its diversity. But, since they are intended to be studied as literature, as well as in performance, they have been chosen because, in the opinion of the writer, they are good examples of their kind.

All of the plays, to the author's certain knowledge, have been successfully performed in public by schoolchildren; many of them, of course, have been set for examination purposes. It is not an accident that the majority of them are modern, for it is modern drama which the pupils are most likely to encounter outside school, and to be interested in. At the same time, tradition is represented by Shakespeare, Ibsen and Shaw, and by the inclusion of plays based on legend, folk-material, or historical fact.

Twelve plays (three of them short ones) cannot possibly cope with the variety of material available. There is, for example, no "Comedy of Manners" of the Restoration or the eighteenth century, nor is there a specimen of the "drawing-room comedy" of the 1930s, since it was felt that the social atmosphere, and the language used, were somewhat rarified. The need to introduce an entirely new theatrical convention accounts for the omission of Greek drama; and certain familiar classics, as well as the more obvious Shakespeare plays, have been omitted on the grounds that many pupils will have come across them already.

I have not restricted my choice in any way to works by play-wrights whose first language is English, but in choosing plays by European dramatists I have been influenced to some extent by the existence—or otherwise—of a good translation.

TERM ONE

Three one-act plays

Fool's Errand by MARGARET WOOD
Sunday Costs Five Pesos by JOSEPHINA NIGGLI
The Happy Journey by THORNTON WILDER

1. Fool's Errand

by MARGARET WOOD

(*This play is a re-telling, in verse, of one of the most famous stories in Chaucer's* Canterbury Tales. *You will remember that, in Chaucer's work, each pilgrim on the road to Canterbury was asked to tell a story, to help to pass the tedious journey. Some of the stories were comic, some very long and full of moral teaching, and some were not even finished; but it is generally agreed that this one, told by the Pardoner, is a masterpiece. It is highly dramatic; it is short, and very economical, in that no words, or characters, are wasted; and it cries out to be made into a play. In fact, this is not the first acting version of the story: there is a Scottish setting of it by James Bridie.*

Margaret Wood, the author of this play, has written a number of successful short plays. Not all of them are based, like this one, on stories from the past; indeed, one of her best-known plays, The Guilty Generation, *is a grimly realistic play about the after-effects of a nuclear war.*)

Story into play

Many old and famous stories will make excellent plays. Shakespeare knew this, and—like many other writers of his day— he borrowed the plots for almost every play he wrote. Some of them came from history, English, Greek, or Roman; and some came from old tales that had been told, countless times, many generations before the plays based on them.

The same, of course, applies to stories from the Bible, and particularly the parables, because they were short, full of action, and simple enough to appeal to a not very educated audience. Furthermore, in medieval times the more familiar biblical stories *had* to be dramatised, so that the ordinary people, ignorant of the Latin used in church, could see for themselves what the life of Christ was really like. Thus it came about that, in the

35

fourteenth century, in cities like York, Chester, Wakefield and
Lincoln, stories from the Bible were acted in the streets before
large crowds of people. They were a huge success not surprisingly,
when you think how dramatic some of them could be—Judas
betraying Christ; the tense moment when the people choose
Barabbas; the temptation in the wilderness; the cleansing of the
temple; and many others.

If you try to turn one of these stories into an improvised play,
with short, effective scenes, you will quickly understand what a
dramatist's problems are. What is exciting enough to read as a
story is sometimes curiously flat when it is performed, because the
conflict in the characters is not there. Take that famous parable,
"The Prodigal Son". In the first scene, the young man wishes to
leave home to seek his fortune, and the scene ends with his
departure. But, to make it interesting, we need perhaps a
mother who begs him to stay, and a father who is willing to let
him go. We also need to introduce the brother, because he
becomes very important later on, when the prodigal returns.
Scene two shows us something of his wasteful life. It cannot show
all of it, and so we need a scene which is *typical* of his wild
behaviour. It should be, perhaps, a tavern scene (an opportunity
for a crowd of actors and actresses, showing the kind of low
company he now keeps), leading up to the discovery that his
money is all gone, and his new "friends" with it. Scene three
shows us his return; and here the most important character is the
brother, who at first resents his welcome home, but is persuaded
to change his mind.

In making a play out of a story, some characters have to be
left out, others made more prominent. A great deal of the detail
of the original story is ignored, so that the action can concentrate
on the main events. At the same time, there must be what is
usually called "background"—that is, something (like the tavern
scene mentioned above) to show what kind of people these are.

Here is the story of the Pardoner, very briefly, as Chaucer
told it:

> Three revellers were drinking in a tavern, when they heard the sound of
> a passing bell, which told them that someone had died in the neighbour-
> hood. There had been many deaths, it seems, of the plague; and the three
> drunken rioters, enraged by the loss of so many good strong fellows,

resolved to go out in search of Death, determined to kill him when they found him. Out they went, and after some time, walking a quiet country path, they came across an old man. They seized him roughly, and asked if he could tell them where Death was hiding. The old man said he wished he could, because in his painful old age he had wished for Death many times, but he was still left to drag his weary body about the earth. Death refused to come to his aid: but, he added, he thought the men might find him under a tree some little way into the nearby wood. The three men followed his guidance, and found, under the tree, a huge quantity of gold coins. They at once forgot their hunt for Death, and resolved to share the spoils. Being unable to move the loot before nightfall, they drew lots to decide who should go back to the town for more ale, while the other two made the division. The youngest went off for the drink; the other two resolved to kill him on his return, and take his share. Meanwhile the third man had had similarly greedy thoughts, and he obtained poison with which he laced the drink intended for the other two. Both pieces of treachery worked according to plan: the youngest was killed, the other two died of the poisoned drink. The three men had set out to look for Death, and they found him, just where the old man told them.

The setting of the story

Chaucer's tale is a fourteenth-century one; and, although there is nothing in the story to prevent it from being transferred to another time, Margaret Wood has decided to keep the medieval setting. This is a good idea, for several reasons: in those days there was much ignorant superstition, and it does not surprise us when three drunken bullies set out to kill "Death" as if he were a human being; then, with disease and violence less easily held in check, human life was cheaper than it is now, and people went in fear of death from quite an early age. The story is a savage one, and it seems to fit the setting very well.

You will notice that the original tale moves from the inn to the countryside. Changes of scene break up the action of a short play, and so Margaret Wood has put the whole play into one *multiple* setting—that is to say, she has one side of the stage representing the outside of the inn, with benches and stools grouped by the door; across the back of the stage runs a fence or hedge, with a stile in it, leading to the wood (and the tree under which the money is found). Thus the whole story can be acted without the need for a change of scene or the drop of a curtain. By moving the drinking scene to *outside* the inn she avoids the necessity for a change of scene.

To keep the medieval flavour of the story, the playwright has done one more thing: she has written it in verse—not the solemn verse of Shakespeare, but a simple kind of rhyming verse, with short lines. This makes the play go at a great speed, as befits the impulsive behaviour and hot tempers of the main characters. There is, of course, a danger that the lines will sound childish and sing-song; but most of the time the lines are cleverly split up amongst the characters so that the danger is overcome. Here, for example, is the moment in the play where the bullies find the money:

OLD MAN: Death lurketh near; not six or seven
Short paces into yonder wood
I left him. May he do you good.
DICCON: So near? God's truth! Suppose he heard
The oaths we've uttered, every word.
Will he not be prepared?
OLD MAN: Not he.
Death was asleep, beneath that tree (*pointing*),
That oak, there on the left, when I
Last saw him.
DICCON: Make no sound or cry
But step full warily, daggers out,
And when I give a mighty shout
Rush on the knave and stab him deep.
Now, brothers, soft behind me creep.
HODGE: (*off*) Now! Strike him down! Strike for your life!
CUDDY: Death's a hard victim! Here's my knife
With steel blade crumpled like a rag.
HODGE: (*dragging a sack with him*) Pox on you, Cuddy, pull this bag
With us; it's such a lump of lead
We can scarce shift it.
CUDDY: Is he dead?
HODGE: Is who dead?
CUDDY: Death?
HODGE: You're stupified.
Death wasn't there. The greybeard lied.
The only thing beneath the tree
Was this great sack . . . Now let me see
What lies inside it.
DICCON: It's so old
It shreds apart . . .
HODGE: Look, brothers!
DICCON: }
CUDDY: }   GOLD!

The plot and the characters

In this acting version, we meet the main characters (the three revellers) as they make merry outside the tavern with Alison (the landlady), Margery and Bet. They flirt with the women, and Diccon leads them in an old song, "Bring us in good ale". Their singing and dancing are at their rowdiest when the sound of the bell cuts across their jollity. But already we have learnt a lot about them: Hodge is the leader, the most drunken, and the noisest; Diccon, more sensible, but content to follow Hodge's lead; and Cuddy, much younger than the others, but a boaster—and (if Alison speaks the truth) not above trying to get away without paying his share.

The determination to kill Death is neatly handled here. The men boast that their old friend, Miller Hugh, could easily deal with Death; and when Margery tells them that it is Miller Hugh who has died they refuse to believe her, and then swear that, if she speaks true, they will avenge Hugh's death themselves. Thus the women leave them; they set off to Hugh's lodgings and are met by the Old Man, who sits on the stile barring their way.

The story follows Chaucer closely up to the finding of the gold. But now the idea of "thieves falling out" is made very clear in the action. Diccon tries to send Cuddy for a cart to carry the money in, and Hodge adds that he might bring some beer at the same time. But Cuddy protests that he is tired of being the errand boy; he doesn't trust the other two to divide the money equally; and he actually grabs a handful of the gold coins, but is stopped by Diccon as he does so. This little quarrel *prepares* the audience for the final treachery, in which the three villains are responsible for each other's deaths.

You can see how, by adding action and character, Margaret Wood has turned this story into an effective play. But one of her most striking effects is a *visual* one—that is, something seen by the audience, but not acted or spoken. At the beginning, before the inn-door opens and the drunken party comes tumbling out, we see the motionless figure of the Old Man, in silhouette against the sky, as he crouches on the stile. We hear him speak, as the three men ask him about Death. And, right at the end, as Hodge and Diccon realise they are poisoned, we see him again, a sinister cloaked figure, at the back of the stage. Hodge, at his last gasp, clutches at the Old Man's cloak, and the hood falls back to reveal the skull of a "death's head". Death has claimed three more victims; the Old Man, and Death, have become the same character.

Two scenes from the play

(1) (from DICCON "Let's sing of ale, boys..." /p. 42 of Best One-Act Plays B.O.A.P. of '58/59/ to Exit of the women /p. 45, *op. cit.*/)

(2) (from HODGE "By God's own might . . ." /p. 52, *op. cit.*/ to end of play).

2. Sunday Costs Five Pesos

by JOSEPHINA NIGGLI

(*This little comedy is from a collection of folk-plays set in the villages and countryside of Mexico. It tells the story of a lovers' quarrel. Fidel is a woodcarver, and wants to get on in the world. So, when he hears that Don Nimfo Garcia will want two handsome carved doors for the new church he is building, he does a bit of serious talking to Celestina, Don Nimfo's daughter. Berta, Fidel's fiancée, is jealous of Celestina, and she and Fidel quarrel. Berta's friends, Tonia and Salome, try to help, and so does Celestina; Fidel gets his wood-carving job, and the lovers "live happily ever after".*

This play has been acted countless times since it was first produced in 1936. Even better known is Josephina Niggli's one-act farce, The Red Velvet Goat, *which tells the story of a very "amateur" performance of a play in a Mexican village.*)

The background to the play

This is a light-hearted and amusing bit of nonsense, but it is impossible to get the best out of it without the realisation that the people in the story live different lives from most of us. In many ways they are just like everybody else, in that they have all the usual feelings of love and jealousy; they quickly lose their tempers and quickly find them again; and, like most people in love, they are most ridiculous when they think they are being tragic. On the other hand, they are very *simple* people—it takes very little to upset them, and very little to make them happy again. Then, since they do not live in a block of flats, or on a suburban housing estate, they can shout at each other, or even have a fight in the street, without losing dignity. Like most simple people, they say just what they think, without worrying about tact or politeness. They are also very *innocent* people, and their lives are ruled by the

41

fear of offending against the code, and therefore losing respect. Berta doesn't mind a scene, or even a fight; but she is horrified at the thought of anyone calling her "improper" in any way. In a small village, where everyone knows everyone else's business, the slightest breath of scandal is a serious matter. One must respect the Church, and guard one's reputation. That is why "Sunday costs five pesos"—in other words, there is a fine for anyone who fights on a Sunday.

This is—in a way—a love story, but it has no love-making. It is obvious that, in the Mexican village of this play, courtship is a very gentle affair. To stroll in the plaza (public square) in the evening, to talk through a window or a doorway, and to sit under the eagle eye of a suspicious parent—these represent the limits of contact with the intended spouse. For instance:

> FIDEL: That is why I came to speak to you. Sit down here on the step with me for a moment.
> BERTA: And have Salome and Tonia say that I am a wicked, improper girl!

The setting of the play

The old Italian comedies were nearly always set in an open square, where several streets met, or where the fronts of several houses could be seen. In this way, all the action could take place in one spot, and the characters could come and go to and from the houses, or from other places in the neighbourhood. This play follows the same pattern: the scene includes the front door and window of Berta's house, with the porch and a strip of street in front of it, while on either side we see the front doors of Salome's and Tonia's houses. In the centre of the stage is a well, and this marks a popular meeting-place for the people of the village.

The language of the play is exactly suited to the characters—it is simple, lively, and expressive. The writer has tried to give it a slight touch of "difference" without making it at all strange or unrealistic. Here is a neat little quarrel scene: notice how it builds up to a climax, with Berta's beautiful final line:

> FIDEL: Do you doubt me, pearl of my life?
> BERTA: Does the rabbit doubt the snake? Does the tree doubt the lightning? Do I doubt that you are a teller of tremendous lies? Speak not to me of cleverness. I know what my eyes see, and I saw you flirting with the Celestina. Last night I saw you . . . and so did all the world!

FIDEL: So that is how you trust me, your intended husband.
BERTA: I would rather trust a hungry fox.
FIDEL: Let me speak plainly, my little dove. Because we are to be married is no reason for me to enter a monastery.
BERTA: And who says that we are to be married?
FIDEL: Why . . . I said it.
BERTA: Am I a dog to your heel that I must obey your every wish?
FIDEL: You are my future wife.
BERTA: Am I indeed?
FIDEL: Your mother has consented, and my father has spoken. The banns have been read in the church!
BERTA: Better to die without children than to be married to such as you!
FIDEL: We shall be married within the month.
BERTA: May this hand rot on my arm if I ever sign the marriage contract.
FIDEL: Are you saying that you will not marry me?
BERTA: With all my mouth I am saying it, and a good day to you.
(*She steps inside, slamming the door. Then immediately opens it.*)
Tell that good news to that four-nosed shrew of a Celestina.

The plot and the characters

The play starts on a high note, with Berta and Fidel quarrelling. We soon know why; and Fidel's excuse—that Celestina was merely a contact for his wood-carving prospects—cuts no ice with Berta. Fidel, disgusted, tells Tonia and Salome that he is through with women, and so it is up to them to try to make Berta see reason. They pretend that Berta has fallen into the well and injured herself, and the news brings poor Fidel running to hear the worst. The scheme might have worked, but for the arrival of Celestina, blazing with anger at being called names by Berta, and demanding revenge. Fidel stalks away when he discovers Berta's trick to get him back, and Berta comes out to meet her deadly rival.

Only the fact that "Sunday costs five pesos" keeps the two girls apart. Salome suggests that they play the old game of "fingers" to decide who strikes the first blow, and therefore pays the fine. Tonia is judge; Salome, supposedly watching to see if Celestina cheats, tries to signal to Berta. Celestina, furious, turns on her and they have a splendid fight—which Celestina wins. It is now Salome's turn to be angry. She threatens to beat up both Berta and Tonia (not on Sunday, of course) for not coming to her assistance. So it is perhaps a good thing that Fidel comes back, with the news that he has got the job from Don

Nimfo Garcia, and that they can be married the following day—
Monday—before Salome has time to carry out her threat.

The central character of the play is, of course, Berta. She has a
superb line in insults, and is quite merciless to poor Fidel; the
only trouble is, she is inclined to let her real feelings get the better
of her. Salome is the managing type, sharp-tongued and tough,
while little Tonia, who means well, is really not a lot of help.
Fidel is a good partner for Berta; he has a habit of asserting
himself, only to come crawling back again a few minutes later.
Celestina has one tremendous battle-scene, and that is all.

Two scenes from the play

Nothing less than the whole play gives the real flavour of this
comedy. However, the scene after Fidel's first exit gives a neat
study of the three girls.

    (1) (from SALOME "Berta!" /p. 13 of French's Acting Edition/
        to SALOME "And what a beautiful idea it is!" /p. 17, *op. cit.*/)

The second scene is the scene with Celestina. It is excellent for
its use of comic gesture and movement as the girls play "fingers"
—all the while highly suspicious of each other.

    (2) (from CELESTINA "I ask you again:" /p. 20 of F.A.E./
        to CELESTINA "So I cheat, eh?" /p. 22/).

3. The Happy Journey

by THORNTON WILDER

(*Most plays have a carefully-planned story leading to a definite conclusion, but this play has no plot. Instead, it shows an ordinary American family—mother, father, and two children—travelling by car to see a married relative who has been ill. The characters are so ordinary that you would hardly notice them in the street, in a restaurant, or on holiday. There are no minor characters, all their parts being read from the script by the Stage Manager. There is no scenery, although there are three scenes: in the first, a bare stage represents a house; in the second, four chairs represent a motor car; and in the third, a camp bed represents all the furniture of another house. And there are no "properties" in this play. The characters carry imaginary suitcases, look through windows that are not there, and "imagine" a whole worldful of objects which only they can see.*

Thornton Wilder is an American who began by writing one-act plays on this sort of pattern. In The Long Christmas Dinner *ninety years pass in less than forty minutes; in* Pullman Car Hiawatha *he allows us to listen to the lives of a large number of people as they sit on the row of ordinary wooden chairs which represent the berths of an express train. His first long play,* Our Town, *is just like this one in the way it is written. In* The Skin of Our Teeth *he tells "the history of the world in comic strip". In his last play,* The Matchmaker, *the characters frequently step outside the play to talk to the audience.*)

Why is the play written like this?

You might try to answer this question for yourselves. Did he do away with scenery, do you think, so that his play could move more easily from place to place? But most audiences *like* a bit of scenery (some audiences, especially those brought up on Hollywood epics, like a lot of scenery), so why not write a play which stayed in one place, and then the scenery could be there as well?

Did he do away with properties, do you think, because most people know what a suitcase looks like, and so they can easily imagine it? Very well; but don't actors look a bit odd, walking about pretending to be carrying bags, and opening doors, and riding in an automobile? Do you think he wrote his play for a company that was short of actors? Otherwise, why have some parts played in full, and others read from the book? Finally, why write the play at all? There is no excitement: four people travel from Newark to Camden, but there is no story, and nothing happens to them—except that they arrive.

When you have tried to answer these problems, it might be a good idea to let Thornton Wilder answer them. In 1958 he wrote this: "Towards the end of the 'twenties I began to lose pleasure in going to the theatre. I ceased to believe in the stories I saw presented there." This—the 'twenties—was a period when scenery was expensive, costumes were gorgeous, and stage effects were new and breathtaking. What Thornton Wilder objected to was not the plays themselves, many of which he read and enjoyed; but the attempts to put them over with all the trappings of everyday life—what he calls ". . . the childish attempt to be 'real' ". So now we have the answer to our first question: he leaves out the scenery and the properties because they are not important, and because they distract our attention away from the people in the play. Or, as he says: "Our claim, our hope, our despair are in the mind—not in things, not in scenery."

But if he wants us to concentrate on the *people* in his plays, then he has to make the people specially interesting. He does this, not by creating kings or noblemen, politicians or artists, but by making his characters recognisable to the ordinary people in the audience. All Thornton Wilder's plays are about "the people next door"—ordinary people, people we know. And ordinary people do not need scenery, or special costume in order to be recognised. That is why, too, he uses the "Stage Manager" (this character appears in at least three of Wilder's plays)—not to save actors, but to allow us to focus on the ones which matter.

That leaves one question still unanswered. Why is there no real "plot"? Thornton Wilder would probably say that his plays are about *life*; that they are "true to life"; and that the lives of most people do not often contain startling or sensational events. To use his own words, he is trying ". . . to find a value above all price for the smallest events in our daily life."

When this play was first performed, it was called *The Happy Journey to Trenton and Camden*; nowadays it is more often simply called *The Happy Journey*. Can you see why the title was changed?

The story and the characters

It is not quite true to say that the play has no plot. It tells the story of the journey, by car, of the Kirby family to the house of the married daughter, Beulah. Beulah has been ill; but Wilder keeps us waiting till almost the end of the play before he tells us just what was the matter. Mrs Kirby has a word of warning to the children as they approach their destination; and we are given a hint—no more—that Beulah has had a "sorta operation".

A little later on, when the "men" have been packed off to the Y.M.C.A. and Caroline is outside playing with the puppies, mother and daughter go upstairs together. Now Beulah remembers how awful it was, having a baby which died; and Ma Kirby remembers how delirious and ill Beulah was. But it is all over now; and "God thought best".

This is, in a way, the climax of the play. At the beginning we have seen the Kirby family preparing for their journey, and the scene is full of little familiar touches: Arthur can't find his cap, Father is fixing the car, Mother is saying goodbye to her neighbours and making quite sure at the same time that they know where she is going and why, and Caroline is "talking to the Jones girls" at the back door. As the house has no walls, no windows and no doors, we can see all these things happening at once. As they troop off the stage for a moment with their baggage, the Stage Manager quickly places four chairs on the stage, and the Kirbys climb into their car and set off.

The journey is full of incident. The car stops for a moment as a funeral procession passes; then Arthur is "naughty" and his mother threatens to send him back home. The car stops at a filling station (with the Stage Manager playing the part of the garage mechanic), and, a little farther on, it stops again while the family buy refreshments from a roadside stall. To pass the time, they sing a little; and, as dusk closes in, Caroline sees the first star, and makes a wish. They almost miss the road to Camden;

then, with the help of Beulah's letter, they find the street, and see Beulah standing on the steps looking out for them.

What makes the journey really interesting, though, is the way the characters describe the scene for us. The children—being children—notice everything: they read the advertisement billboards, the posters, the signposts. Mother, on the other hand, is happy because they are out of the town and into the country, smelling the clean air, and she admires the fine buildings of the various places they pass through. Father, intent on his driving, jokes quietly with the children; and, although he talks little, and his wife talks a great deal, we can feel the tremendous respect the whole family has for him. At the end of this journey, we feel we know these people very well indeed.

Two scenes from the play

When you have read the whole play through, it might be an interesting experiment to imagine the characters *before* the play begins. Imagine, for instance, the breakfast scene when Beulah's letter arrives, and try to make up the conversation. Or, for a change, go to the end of the play: what kind of a person do you think Horace, Beuiah's husband, is? You might make up a little scene in which he comes home from work and meets the Kirby family.

These two scenes from the play are both taken from the actual "journey": the first one takes us up to Arthur's quarrel with his mother, and the second is the arrival at Beulah's house.

(1) (from ARTHUR "Pa! Pa! Don't go by the school" /p. 96, Eight One-Act Plays, Nelson, 1961/
   to MA "I don't want to talk about it" /p. 100, *op. cit.*/).

(2) (from CAROLINE "I see the first star" /p. 104, E.O.A.P./
   to BEULAH "Go and see' /p. 106, *op. cit.*/.)

TERM TWO

Two stories from the past

Noah by ANDRÉ OBEY
The Caucasian Chalk Circle by BERTOLT BRECHT

1. Noah

by ANDRÉ OBEY

(This famous play was first produced in 1931, and received its first performance in English in 1935. Since then it has been produced many hundreds of times, by both professional and amateur companies; it has been a favourite play of school drama groups; and it has probably been performed more often than any other modern play on a Biblical theme. One of the reasons for its success is that it was specially written for a company of young actors working with a very talented director, Jacques Copeau, who trained his actors to create the drama without the aid of elaborate stage settings. The play is full of movement, because the characters all express their feelings by moving about freely; and the language of the play is very simple, because the playwright wants us to share the simple feelings of these very ordinary people.

André Obey's best-known plays, apart from Noah, *are* The Rape of Lucrece, *(which was made into an opera by Benjamin Britten) and* The Battle of the Marne. *So you can see that Obey usually turns to events of the past to provide the material for his plots.)*

An idea for a story

We have already seen, in the short play *Fool's Errand*, how a good story can be turned into an exciting play simply by following the story closely, and making only slight changes in transforming the story into something suitable to be acted. But in the case of *Noah* things are very different. If you read the story as it appears in the Old Testament, it contains scarcely any detail that could be useful in a play. The Bible tells us a lot about the size of the Ark, and the number and variety of the animals, the depth of the flood waters, and the duration of the flood before the waters receded. We are told the names of Noah's three sons, and—in a later chapter—we are told how Noah quarrelled with Ham, and placed a curse upon his descendants. Of the actual circumstances of the building of the Ark, of the behaviour of the people cooped up in it for so long, we are told nothing. So, to make the play, Obey has to *invent* the characters, and the details of the story, keeping just the bare outline of the story that we all know from the Bible.

You will remember that, in the Bible account, Noah sent out a raven from the Ark to see if the waters were sinking, and he also sent a dove—three times in all—for the same reason. Obey keeps this idea of the dove, and builds one of his most important scenes round it, but he sends the bird only once. Then, although the play stops shortly after the Ark comes to rest, Obey uses the idea contained in the Bible that Ham was a troublesome son. In the play, Ham is used as a rebel, as somebody who is impatient of the old man and his ways. This helps to make the play more interesting. But, apart from these small details, Obey has not taken a Bible story and retold it as a play; he has used the original as "an idea for a play"—all the rest is his own invention.

I suppose you could say that, while the bare bones of the story are provided by Genesis, Chs. 6–9, the flesh and blood, the human feeling, the brain and the heart of the matter, are provided by the playwright. Obey is not really interested in the size and shape of the Ark, or the kind of wood of which it was constructed, or the precise number of living creatures which it was designed to accommodate; but he is interested in how people—real people, not just names in a book—would act, and feel, and think, if they found themselves adrift in a wooden box for months on end.

Using an ancient myth

Obey does something very surprising to the Bible story as we know it. He makes the three sons—Ham, Shem, and Japhet— very young; and, instead of taking their wives with them, the three boys take three young girls, casual acquaintances who turn up just before the Ark sails, who have as yet no idea that they are going to be the mothers of new races of human beings.

Why does Obey make all his characters (except for Mr. and Mrs. Noah) so young? I think because young people are more excitable, quickly filled with pleasure or disappointment, very changeable, and very easily led by someone with a strong personality. And, in a way, the trouble that develops on the Ark is a kind of war between age, wisdom and trust on the one hand, and eagerness, rebellion, and impatience on the other. Another thing—young people are soon bored and discontented, and this long, tedious journey over the watery deserts is very hard and trying for them. We can sympathise with them when they are restless and bored; and we can share their enthusiasm when something really good happens.

If you read a bit of the play, you will see that, as with so many myths, the language is so simple, so childlike, that it reads just like the simple wording of a children's book; but, once you start to act the scenes, remembering that the actors would not stand still, but would move about to the rhythm of the words, you can see how effective the language is in showing us the *feelings* of the characters. Here is an example. The Ark has come to land at last, and the children have seen the earth for the first time for many months. This is the scene, and these are the words the author uses. It is true that nobody would ever talk like this, but that does not matter, provided the words help the actors to create the mood for the audience:

ALL: Ah!
BOYS: Aha!
GIRLS: Haha!
          (*They are all lined up before the Ark.*)
HAM: Ha! Old Earth!
BOYS: Good old Earth!
GIRLS: Dear old Earth!
JAPHET: (*Stepping out of line*). Look! I'm going to walk! Watch me walk! What am I doing?
ALL: Walking!
JAPHET: What's this boy doing?
ALL: He's walking!
JAPHET: Walking where?
ALL: On the ground!
NAOMI: (*getting out of line*) Look at me! Look at me! (*She pulls up her skirts to her knees.*)
ADA: }
SELLA:}   Look at us.
NAOMI: I'm squelching in the mud.
ADA: }
SELLA:}   We're squelching too.
BOYS: Let's all squelch.
HAM: It's wet!

JAPHET: It's cold!
SHEM: But it's warming up under our feet.
BOYS: It's soft! It feels so good!
ALL: One, two! One, two!
NAOMI: Look! My feet are all black!
ALL: One, two! One, two!
HAM: (*getting out of line.*) Be quiet!
ALL: One, two!
HAM: Shut up! Shut up! (*Pause*). I want to feel that at last—I'm really *free*!

Now, try to picture the scene for yourself. The stage is bare, but for the prow of the Ark just visible at the side, near the back of the stage; and there is a small mound of earth, represented perhaps by a couple of shallow boxes with a painted cloth thrown over it. Using just this setting, the six boys and girls have to show us what it feels like to be on dry land again. They stand for a moment in delighted amazement—remember, they never thought they would see dry land in their whole lives, once the flood waters had come. Then, perhaps, they crouch down and feel the soft ground with their fingers, as they whisper the words "Good old Earth" and "Dear old Earth"; then they start to walk, slowly at first (still unsteady on their legs after the sea voyage), and gradually faster and faster, until they are all squelching about like three-year-old children allowed out after a storm of rain, and shouting at the tops of their voices. Ham, of course, is not content with this, and he breaks out of line to "show off"—like a little child again. But to do this he has to shout down the others, who for the moment are so absorbed that they do not hear him. There is not mud on the stage, and the actors who play these six parts are not children; but it is not difficult, using these words and these movements, to make the audience believe in the scene.

Just as the language is simple, so also is the presentation. Obey cannot possibly build us the Ark, nor can he show us all the creatures which went into it, so he does not try. There are eight animals in the play, and they will do to represent all the others. In the first and last scenes we see a bit of the Ark, just enough to let us imagine the rest of it; and the other scenes take place on the deck (for which an empty stage will do) or in the cabin.

It seems obvious that the main character of the play is Noah himself. He is not a child, and he does not talk in quite the same language as the other, younger characters, but he is a simple man, and he has a simple trust in God. He is, Ham thinks, too simple; and sometimes we find him slightly comic. Here he is, right at the beginning of the play: and you will see from this speech how, from the start, Obey uses simple, almost childlike, language. Hamlet says: "An old man is twice a child"—and there is something very childlike about Noah:

> NOAH (*softly*): Lord . . . (*louder*) Lord . . . (*Very loud*) Lord! . . . Yes, Lord, it's me. Extremely sorry to bother you again, but . . . What's that? Yes, I know You've other things to think of, but after I've shoved off won't it be a little late? . . . Oh, no, Lord, no, no, no . . . No, Lord, please don't think that . . . Oh, but naturally, of course I trust You! You could tell me to set sail on a plank—a branch—on just a cabbage leaf . . . Yes, You could even tell me to put out to sea with nothing but my loincloth, even without my loincloth, completely—
> (*He has gone down on his knees, but gets up again immediately.*)
> Yes, yes, Lord, I beg Your pardon. I know Your time is precious. Well, this is all I wanted to ask You: Should I make a rudder? I say, a rudder . . . No, no, Lord. R for Robert; U for Una; D for . . . that's it, a rudder. Good . . . very good, I never thought of that. Of course, winds, currents, tides . . . What was that, Lord? Storms? Oh, and while You're there, just one other little thing . . . Are you listening, Lord? (*To the audience*) Gone!! . . . He's in a bad temper . . . Well, you can't blame Him; He has so much to think about. All right; no rudder.

This amusing speech tells us a lot about Noah; but it is also quite important to the story. Noah realises from this that God will steer the Ark, and nobody else, but he has a hard job to convince his children that this is the way it should be.

The plot of the play

As we said earlier, many things happen in this play which are not even mentioned in the Bible narrative, and they are all put into the story quite deliberately.

Scene One opens with the speech you have just read. Then the animals come, but, instead of fighting, they all move placidly into the Ark. The children come running, and two of them go back to bring Mrs Noah, while Noah explains to them what he has been building. Excitedly the boys climb all over it; and then the three girls, who have been following a cat, arrive on the scene. They do not know why they are here, but they have a feeling that some danger threatens them. Noah understands why they have come, and he is just going to tell all of them what it is about when a man appears from the undergrowth. He accuses Noah of stealing the animals, and of being responsible for the terrible drought. He threatens the old man with a spear; Noah calls on God to prove he is right, and splashes of rain begin to fall. The light fades; the children revel in the cool drops, but the man tries to dodge them; the man sinks down under the falling torrent; the thunder rolls; the family enter the Ark.

Scene Two is six weeks later, in the cabin on the Ark. Read this scene carefully because it shows how much real drama there can be made out of eight people just waiting. First we see them talking about the storm, doing their chores, wondering if they will ever see the dry earth again. The climax of this section is when Noah describes how he saw the last human beings, on the highest mountain tops, perishing in the flood. Then the girls realise why they are there, and we get the beginning of the courtship between Ham and Naomi which will eventually lead to the three sons of Noah taking wives. And then, something tremendous happens: the rain stops, and the sun comes out, and the scene ends in a burst of joy and excitement.

Scene Three shows us again how like children we all are. The young people are getting bored with the journey, and they are trying to catch fish. But also—led by Ham—they are getting discontented, rebellious. Ham is growing up, getting impatient; and he suddenly sounds much more "modern";

> Ham: That's what I said. Oh, I've kept count all right. Five months of water, of animals, of each other! Five months of waiting—and, my God, we don't even know what for! I tell you it's driving me crazy! And the old man doesn't do anything—he doesn't do a thing—not a single thing.

To amuse themselves, they begin to torment the animals, but Noah appears and puts a stop to this. The scene ends with Noah trying to explain to the animals that the children are not really wicked; but, every time Ham's name is mentioned, the animals growl their disapproval.

Scene Four brings the rebellion to a head. A powerful wind is blowing, and Ham is urging the others to help him to erect a sail so that they can steer the Ark. The others, even including Mrs. Noah, are beginning to form up against the old man. He sends out the dove, and for a moment or two they are fascinated by this; but they are ready to take command of the Ark, in spite of Noah, rather than wait for the dove to come back. As the dove returns, Ham and his father come to blows: but the dove has brought the olive branch, and they are safe.

Scene Five is very short. We are at last on dry land, and the scene begins with the passage we quoted earlier, where the children rush about for joy on the newly-revealed Earth. They then begin to squabble among themselves, the boys fighting to be "top dog"; but the girls notice that the animals are all heading for the plains and valleys below, and the three pairs of children set off to follow them—Ham and Naomi to the south; Shem and Sella to the east; and Japhet and Ada to the west. They go to found the great races of the world, the black, the yellow, and the white. The old man is left alone with Mrs Noah, and now not even his old friends the wild animals are friendly any more. And this is how the play ends:

NOAH: . . . it's a good thing I have such trust in You . . . Do You hear? I'll say You've given me some pretty hard knocks. It's been a bit past a joke sometimes, I can tell You! You take me from my garden and chuck me on a bare rock, all by myself, with a hundred ways of dying . . . Haha! . . . All right, all right. Don't You worry. I'll find a way out, somehow or other. I'll find a way out all right! I tell You frankly I've given up trying to understand. But no matter. Go on, I'm following You! Oh, let's go on! Only just one thing I'd like to ask You. Be up there a bit just now and again, will You? Just let me hear Your voice once in a while, or feel Your breath, just see Your light, even. Lord, if You'd just shed Your light on my work as I do it every day, and give the *feeling*—the *assurance*—the conviction that You are satisfied. We must all be satisfied, mustn't we? Well, I am satisfied. (*He shouts*) I am satisfied! (*He sings*) Are You satisfied?
(*The seven colours of the rainbow appear in the background.*)
That's fine!

Something to think about

This play illustrates one of the miracles of the theatre. It starts from one of the oldest stories in the world, a story which

3

most people regard as a legend; and, with the simplest of scenery, in language that everyone can follow, and with only a handful of characters, who rely so much on the audience's use of imagination, it makes the story seem both exciting and important. Notice how every scene contains, not one, but several climaxes of exciting action; notice, too, how many different moods the scenes express—boredom, fear, panic, impatience, anger, curiosity, joy, and so on; and notice how these moods change, quite suddenly, to make the play constantly interesting. But most important of all, notice how much of "human nature" there is in the play. These characters do not behave like figures from an Old Testament fable, but like people we all know.

Scenes to act from the play

The first scene (like the one in which the children first see land) illustrates the importance of *movement* to express feelings. It comes from Scene ONE, where THE MAN suddenly appears; it ends with the actors *imagining* the first drops of rain falling:

    (1) (from THE MAN ". . . Stop!" /p. 11 of Heinemann ed., 1953/
        to MAMMA, etc ". . . It's raining . . ."/ p. 15, ditto/).

The second scene is one of the most famous in the play. There is no dove, of course, but by concentrating hard, and following the flight of the imaginary bird, the actors make us believe in it. This is the part of Scene FOUR in which Noah sends the bird out of the Ark.

    (2) (from NOAH ". . . Ada, my child" /p. 43 *op. cit.*/
        to NOAH "Results" /p. 45/).

2. The Caucasian Chalk Circle

by BERTOLT BRECHT

(Bertolt Brecht was a German, born in 1898, and most of his plays were written between 1930 and the end of the Second World War. Like Obey, Brecht wanted his plays to appeal to a very wide audience; and so a Brecht play usually has a very clear and exciting story, with many scenes, and the action is almost always based on an old folk-tale, or a piece of history. Brecht, like Obey, had very definite ideas of how his plays should be acted and produced, and he actually founded a company, the Berliner Ensemble, which has continued to produce his plays since his death.

Brecht was a Communist, and the home of his company was, and still is, East Germany. So we would expect to find in his work, not the simple telling of a story, but a powerful argument for the ideas in which he firmly believed. Of course, if the plays merely preached politics at us we should very soon tire of them; but if they also happen to be interesting, amusing, and original, we can enjoy them without necessarily agreeing with all of the author's opinions.

Brecht has retold many an old story—as in Baal, *a modern version of the brutalities of pagan worship: but his best-known plays are probably* The Good Woman of Setzuan *(based, like this one, on an old Chinese legend);* The Threepenny Opera *(based on* The Beggar's Opera *by Gay); and* Mother Courage *(a chronicle play of the Thirty Years' War).)*

"Epic Theatre"

This is the phrase that Brecht himself used to describe the kind of plays he wrote. In many ways it is very appropriate, because most Brecht plays are *big* plays—they tell a big story, they deal with important matters, and they have many scenes, and many characters. Like Shakespeare, Brecht created plays which were larger than life, and in nearly all of them a popular Communist problem—the idea of the *class struggle*—is prominent. In other words, the plays show us the effect on the lives of ordinary people of the behaviour of those in authority. Usually, though not always, the corrupt ones are those who have the power and the influence, who misuse government, and who ill-treat those less fortunate than themselves, while the peasants remain patient and under-privileged, unable to do very much about it. This does not mean that, according to Brecht, all the rich are bad, and the poor and needy are honest and good. He finds selfishness and ignorance in all walks of life, and he does not pretend that poverty is an excuse for vice. But, because of his political views, he often looks at religion, and patriotism, and justice, in an unexpected way. A good story, to Brecht, has two uses: it allows him to fill his stage with varied incidents and colourful characters; and it serves as a kind of parable through which he can say something important about human behaviour.

Some writers, we know, are never likely to be really popular, because not everybody likes their style, or the things they write about. Brecht is just the opposite: he does everything he can to make his plays appeal to a very wide audience, because he wants to get his message to as many people as possible. In a Brecht play there is something for everybody. Firstly, there is always a good story, with plenty of action and excitement; then, even if the idea behind the story is serious, there is always plenty of humour—humour of a simple kind that most people will enjoy. The story is usually told in a series of separate scenes, none of them very long, so that the audience can enjoy the action without getting tired or bored; and the scenes often contain songs, in which the point of the scene is underlined.

Since the stories which Brecht tells are often very long, he has to leave out some of the less important episodes, and so he has to find a way of telling his audience what is happening. So he uses a *narrator* of some kind to keep the story moving. In *Mother Courage* a series of painted banners is used, and these are changed between scenes so that the audience can read a little about the things that have happened off-stage; in *The Good Woman of Setzuan* the story is told by Wong, the water-seller—sometimes to the audience, and sometimes in conversation with the three Gods who keep dropping in to see how the "good woman" is getting along; and in this play Brecht uses a character called, simply, The Storyteller.

It is interesting to compare this play with *Noah*. They both tell an old story, using simple language, and relying upon action and movement rather than upon scenery and stage effect, and their characters are somewhat alike in being straightforward and uncomplicated. On the other hand, while *Noah* is short, with few characters, and very little violent action, *The Chalk Circle* needs several principals, a large number of minor characters, and a crowd of courtiers, soldiers, and common people. Its story is big, sprawling over many miles, and spread over a number of years, and the action is not merely violent, but at times savage and brutal.

Presenting the play

If a play has a number of scenes, a crowd of actors, and plenty of violent movement, it obviously cannot have much scenery. One of the things that Brecht insisted upon was an open stage with plenty of room for movement. The need for scenery is largely disposed of by using a Storyteller, and so the simplest suggestion of furniture and setting is all that is needed. Besides, although the story is set in ancient times, it is meant for *us*, and it would be wrong to make the setting too strange. Parts of the play, in any case, are quite impossible to act without the audience using its imagination. In this play there are soldiers on the march, and at one point the heroine has to struggle across a broken bridge over a raging torrent to escape them. More than once the scene changes from interior to exterior in the middle of an exciting episode, and this alone renders real scenery completely impracticable. (It is interesting to note that, in *Mother Courage*, the frequent journeys with the canteen waggon were suggested by using a revolving stage, so that the waggon remained in more or less the same spot while the scenery—such as it was—moved behind it.)

To Brecht, the *atmosphere* of a play was very important, and in this respect he did some very unexpected things. He was very concerned that the audience should not feel sorry for his characters, because he was more interested in the *idea* behind the play than the people in it; therefore he expected his actors *not* to play for sympathy. You will notice that there are no really good people in this play: some of them do the right things, and some do not, but they all have their faults. Brecht drew them like this on purpose, and he insisted that there should be no sentimentality about them. He also lit his stage very brightly (even when the scene takes place at night) so as to avoid any suggestion of "romantic atmosphere". There is plenty of action, some of it extremely violent, and at times the language is coarse and brutal; there are moments of tenderness and love, but there are no real "love-scenes"—the final impression of the play is that it represents a harsh and unfriendly world.

A Brecht play contains only two kinds of people—the bosses, the rulers, the ones who give the orders; and the poor, the down-trodden, and the destitute. These latter, the peasants who make up the vast majority of the people in the country, are the ones Brecht sympathised with, and they speak the language of ordinary, simple folk. On the other hand, to show us how inhuman a prince or a governor can be, he suggested that these characters should be played in masks, and this practice is some-times followed when his plays are produced. They wear masks because they have no human feelings, no sympathy for those less fortunate than themselves.

The Chalk Circle

Do you remember the story of the judgment of Solomon? There was a dispute between two women, each of whom claimed that a baby belonged to her, and that the other was trying to steal it by claiming it. Solomon could persuade neither of them to change her story, and so he ordered that the baby be cut in half, and that each claimant should be given an equal share. At once one of the women cried out in horror, saying that she would rather lose the child to her rival than see it killed. Solomon decreed that this woman, since she had shown concern for the child's life, must be the true mother.

A similar "judgment" is recorded in a Chinese play of the year 1300. A circle of chalk was drawn on the ground, and the dis-puted child was placed in the centre of it. The two "mothers" were each asked to take an arm, and told to pull the child out of the circle, to one side or the other. The true mother let the child go, preferring to lose the test rather than hurt the child in any way. Thus was the judgment decided, and the child handed over, not to the one who succeeded in pulling him out, but to the one who released her hold upon him. It was this legend which gave Brecht the idea for his play.

The story of the play

"In olden times, in a bloody time,
There ruled in a Causacian city—
Men called it the City of the Damned—
A governor.
His name was Georgi Abashwili.
He was as rich as Croesus
He had a beautiful wife
He had a healthy child.
No other governor in Grusinia
Had so many horses in his stable
So many beggars on his doorstep
So many soldiers in his service
So many petitioners in his courtyard . . ."

The governor and his family are going to church. It is Easter Sunday. The crowds are out, both to lay their complaints before the governor (who ignores them) and to catch a glimpse of the child (a baby in arms, accompanied by a pair of comic doctors). The governor seems unconcerned, and he even refuses to listen to messages from the capital. The crowds mutter about rebellion, but the family go in to the service. Grusha, the kitchen girl, and Simon, the member of the Palace Guard, meet and talk for a few minutes; the stage is empty for a short time; and then there is swift and sudden action. The Fat Prince, brother to the governor, appears, giving orders to the soldiers, and the mutiny is on. The governor is arrested, the palace Guard refusing to defend him, and there is a mad scramble for survival as the palace servants gather what they can. The governor's wife, caring more for her dresses and jewels than for her child, goes off, leaving Grusha with the baby. At the first sounds of trouble, she and Simon have agreed to separate, and to meet—and marry— when the fuss dies down. Now the palace burns, the Fat Prince fixes the governor's head over the gate, and Grusha trudges off with the noble child in her arms.

A string of short but exciting scenes shows us how Grusha escapes with the child. We see her buying milk with her last few coins in order to keep him alive; and then we see two Ironshirts, who have been sent to find the child and bring him back. Grusha meets them, having just abandoned the baby on the doorstep of a small farm, but she makes the mistake of running away, and the soldiers follow. She goes back to the house, and tells the peasant woman to pretend the child is hers. The soldiers, suspicious of the fine clothes the baby is wrapped in, take a closer look; Grusha, in desperation, grabs a log from the hearth, knocks the corporal out, and runs off once more with the child. She reaches a bridge over a gorge, the soldiers only a few minutes behind her, and she manages to stagger across to safety, although the bridge is rotten, and nobody else had dared to make the attempt.

At last she reaches her brother's house. He is glad to see her, and takes her in; but he is worried about the child, afraid of what his wife—and the neighbours—will think. Eventually he persuades Grusha to agree to a "marriage of convenience" with the son of a local peasant woman. The son is dying, anyway, so Grusha won't really have a husband—just a name for the child. This is a riotously funny scene, since there seems to be some doubt in the minds of the guests as to whether they have come to a wedding or a funeral. To make it worse, Grusha and her brother are trying to hide the child from the priest who is to perform the ceremony. When the son makes a miraculous recovery, poor Grusha is landed with a husband she does not want. Eventually, Simon and the other soldiers come for the child (by now a healthy boy of six years), and Simon is horrified to find his wife-to-be has a husband and a child already; and, naturally, he finds it hard to believe that she has been innocent of any deception all this time.

This ends the first part of the play. Notice what a great deal Brecht has packed into three scenes; and notice, too, that with the aid of the Storyteller, and a large, open stage, the play has covered considerable stretches of time and space. Now, in Act II, the action moves back to the starting point—Grusinia.

Hear the story of the judge
How he turned judge, how he passed judgment, what kind of judge he was.
On that Easter Sunday of the great revolt, when the grand duke was overthrown
And his governor Abashwili, father of our child, lost his head
The Village Recorder Azdak found in the woods a fugitive and hid him in his
　　hut . . .

The fugitive is the Grand Duke, and Azdak, though he knows he is an enemy of the poor, has pity on him and saves him from the law. Then, ashamed of himself for letting the side down, he gives himself up to the Ironshirts, and confesses what he has done. Meanwhile, the Fat Prince is anxious to find a job for his nephew, and proposes him as Judge in Grusinia. Azdak agrees to be the accused, so that the court can try out the nephew's skill in law; then, mimicking the Grand Duke, Azdak outsmarts his accuser, and the Ironshirts, enjoying the joke, make Azdak judge instead.

Azdak ruled as judge for two years, and we see several examples of his peculiar "justice". In his crude way, he is doing a good job. He takes money from his clients, but he does not allow it to influence his judgment. He breaks all the rules, but somehow people seem to stand a better chance of a fair settlement than they used to do. But all good things come to an end.

In the last scene, the revolution is over, and all the old, corrupt powers are back in office. The soldiers are once more the servants of the Grand Duke, and the governor's wife, attended by her two lawyers, has come to the court to claim her son, Michael, the child which Grusha took away and has cared for. The soldiers who appointed Azdak are waiting for the name of the new judge; so, to amuse themselves, they are beating Azdak preparatory to hanging him. However, the Grand Duke has not forgotten how Azdak saved his life, and he sends word that Azdak is to continue as judge. And now we come to the case of Grusha, the wife of the dead governor, and the child—and to the Chalk Circle.

Azdak agrees to take two cases at once. The second one concerns an old couple who have been married for years and now want a divorce. Azdak tries the test of the chalk circle, and awards the child to Grusha—the "true mother". He then signs the divorce papers; but, by accident (?) he divorces Grusha and her peasant husband, so that now Simon and she can be married.

And after that evening Azdak disappeared and was not seen again.
The people of Grusinia did not forget him but long remembered
The period of his judging as a brief golden age
Almost an age of justice.
   But you, you who have listened to the story of the Chalk Circle,
Take note what men of old concluded:

That what there is shall go to those who are good for it,
Thus: the children to the motherly, that they prosper;
The carts to good drivers, that they are driven well
And the valley to the waterers, that it brings forth fruit.

The importance of crowds

This is a long play, but it is longer to act than to read. In a number of scenes the important parts are the lines suggested for the crowd to speak, and one can easily imagine the actors inventing lines of their own, in the same manner, to make the scene more realistic:

> BEGGARS AND PETITIONERS: Mercy! Mercy, Your Grace! The taxes are way up, we can't pay!
> —I lost my leg in the Persian War, where can I get . . .
> —My brother is innocent, Your Grace, there's been a misunderstanding . . .
> —The child is starving in my arms!
> —Our petition is for our son's discharge from the army, our last remaining son!
> —Please, Your Grace, the water inspector takes bribes.

A little later on, when the revolution is in progress, and the governor's household is in a state of panic, another crowd—this time the palace servants—appears:

> SERVANTS: The baskets!
> —Take them all into the third courtyard! Food for three days!
> —The mistress has fainted! Someone must carry her down. She must get away.
> —What about us? We'll be slaughtered like chickens, that's how it always is.
> —Goodness gracious, what'll happen? There's bloodshed already in the city, they say.
> —Nonsense, the governor has just been politely asked to appear at a Princes' meeting. Everything'll be ironed out. I heard this on the best authority . . .

The "Neighbours" who attend the farcical wedding scene later in the play are not given lines to speak, but their reactions to the development of the story are quite important. The small group of people standing by the rotten bridge must show, by their fear and distress, the danger which cannot be properly represented on the stage in any other way.

If you look carefully at the crowd scenes in this play, you will notice that they cannot be acted properly unless each actor plays a different character. A crowd is never just a mass of people; look closely at it, and you will see that it is made up of individuals, varying greatly in age, in courage, and in manner of speaking. It is called a crowd because all the members of it speak together; but they do not speak in chorus, nor do they act and speak alike. Try the church scene for yourself. You need a small group to represent the governor's family, walking disdainfully, and ignoring the cries of the crowd; a small bodyguard of soldiers, harsh, brutal, and ruthless; and an assortment of people of all ages and types, but all united in their poverty, their misery, and their hopelessness.

The simplicity of the dialogue

Brecht gets most of his effects, both serious and comic, by very simple means. Here, for instance, are the two sycophantic doctors who attend the royal baby—first, before the revolution:

GOVERNOR'S WIFE: He's coughing, Georgi, did you hear? (*To the doctors*): He's coughing!

FIRST DOCTOR: (*To second*): May I remind you, Niko Mikadze, that I was against the lukewarm bath? There's been a little error in warming the bath water, Your Grace.

SECOND DOCTOR: Mika Loladze, I can't possibly agree with you. The temperature of the bath water was the one prescribed by our great, beloved Mishiko Oboladze. It was more likely a slight draught during the night, Your Grace.

GOVERNOR'S WIFE: But do pay more attention to him. He looks feverish, Georgi.

FIRST DOCTOR: No cause for alarm, Your Grace. The bath water will be warmer. It won't occur again.

SECOND DOCTOR: I won't forget that, my dear Mika Loladze. No cause for concern, Your Grace.

THE FAT PRINCE: Well, well, well! I always say: One pain in my liver and the doctor gets fifty strokes on the soles of his feet.

A few pages later, we meet the doctors again, as they rush into the courtyard during the revolutionary panic:

FIRST DOCTOR: Niko Mikadze, it is your duty as a doctor to attend
                   Natella Abashwili.
SECOND DOCTOR: My duty! It's yours!
FIRST DOCTOR: Whose turn is it to look after the child today, Niko
                   Mikadze, mine or yours?
SECOND DOCTOR: Do you really think, Mika Loladze, I'm going to stay
                   a minute longer in this blasted house on that little
                   brat's account?
                   (*They fight. The second doctor knocks the first one down.*)
SECOND DOCTOR: Oh, go to hell. (*Exit.*)

Much later, just before the judgment of the Chalk Circle, we
meet the Governor's wife again, but this time the comic doctors
have been replaced by comic lawyers. It is amusing to compare
their cunning speeches with the simple honesty of the poor people
who come before Azdak asking for judgment. Simon and Grusha
have no money to bribe the judge with, and there are no fine
clothes to dress the child in. To make matters worse, they
bitterly attack Azdak for being corrupt, and risk losing their case.
But this is a folk-tale; and, like most good folk-tales, it has a
happy ending.

Scenes from the play

The first two scenes show how Brecht creates a feeling of
tenderness and trust by the simplest of means. We first see Simon
proposing to Grusha, in the heat of the revolutionary upheaval:

(1) (from SIMON: "Grusha! There you are . . ." /p. 115 Evergreen Ed./
     to SIMON ". . . waiting my return" /p. 117, *op. cit.*/).

Next we see them when the soldiers come for the child. They are
on opposite sides of a river:

(2) (from GRUSHA: "Simon!" /p. 151, Evergreen Ed./
     to SIMON ". . . the wife need say no more." /p. 153, *op. cit.*/).

Finally, the judgment of the Chalk Circle. The scene is a long
one, and well worth studying complete. Here is the climax of
the scene:

(3) (from AZDAK ". . . I hear you want . . ." /p. 185, Evergreen Ed./
     to AZDAK ". . . I've got forty piasters coming from you." /p. 188, *op.
     cit.*/).

TERM THREE

Two realistic plays

An Enemy of the People by HENRIK IBSEN
The Devil's Disciple by BERNARD SHAW

1. An Enemy of the People

by HENRIK IBSEN

(*Although it was written in 1882, this play will probably seem as modern to you as anything else in this book. The reason is simple: Ibsen was the first dramatist to realise that ordinary people can have to face serious problems, and make weighty decisions; that these crises can occur, quite naturally, as they go about their everyday business; and that, in short, a play does not have to be about princes and prime ministers in order to be interesting. This idea, so very obvious to us, was quite revolutionary in Ibsen's own time. Modern dramatists, however, have eagerly followed Ibsen's lead, with the result that very many of the plays and films we see nowadays reflect the life which goes on around us. Ibsen's realistic plays do rather more than reflect the life of nineteenth-century Norway; they also have something to say about problems of living which are just as real now as they were then.*

This is the last of a group of four plays, written between 1877 and 1882, all dealing with urgent social problems. Pillars of Society *is about a merchant who puts commercial profit above honesty;* A Doll's House *and* Ghosts *both deal, in different ways, with marriage and the emancipation of women.* Ghosts—*probably because it discussed, among other things, the question of hereditary disease—invoked a storm of abusive criticism. (One London newspaper called it ". . . a lazar house with all the doors and windows open.") After the cruel reception given to this play, Ibsen was furious with the stupidity of his audiences. To teach them a sharp lesson, he wrote this play.*

Not all of Ibsen's plays are in this naturalistic style. His earlier plays were vast epics, often in verse, based on some remote historical event, or derived from Scandinavian folk-lore. His last plays, though no longer in verse, are nevertheless filled with poetic symbols, and strange, tragic characters.)

71

"*The Fourth Wall*"

What do we mean by a "realistic" or a "naturalistic" play? We usually mean that the writer has arranged things in such a way that we feel we are looking in on a slice of life. This is not, of course, true of Shakespeare, whose characters speak in verse, and whose scenes change every few minutes. But in a realistic play the stage represents the kind of house, or shop, or farm, or office, that most people in the audience would recognise and be familiar with. The characters are observed going about their ordinary life, greeting their friends, talking to their families, eating supper or breakfast. The stage is made to look so much like the real thing that we in the audience feel we are actually looking into a room from which the fourth wall has been removed.

The way the characters speak must be made to fit in with this idea. They do not break off their conversations to speak with the audience, or to talk to themselves. They do not tell us about themselves, or about the kind of people they are; these things we have to guess at by the clues and hints contained in their talk with each other. On the other hand, we quickly get to know them, because in so many ways they are like people we know. In a sense, we in the audience are *eavesdroppers*, allowed to listen to the private conversations of strangers.

Ibsen was one of the first to write in this way. Although he did it well, others have done it just as convincingly. You will notice, for instance, that the characters in this play are not very complicated, and not very subtle. They repeat themselves rather a lot (as, indeed, we all do when we are excited, or indignant, or enthusiastic about something), and they seem unusually blind to other people's point of view. The hero, Dr. Stockmann, though a brave and fearless man, is also, you might think, rather stupid—and certainly very proud and conceited. Most of the characters, in fact, seem to have only one side to their nature, and Ibsen was wrong to imagine that human beings could be so easily classified. But he had an excuse: it was the ignorant masses, the "compact majority", as he called it, who were the real villains of this play, and I think he made his characters very simple so that the audience could tell at once what they believed in, and what they stood for.

Ibsen's craftsmanship

Most Ibsen plays begin very near the end—that is to say, most of the really important things have already happened before the play begins. Ibsen picks up the story just as something new and startling is about to happen.

He therefore has a neat problem. He has to let us know fairly quickly about the events of the past; and, at the same time, he has to let us bit by bit into the new developments in the present. He also has to give us a fairly clear idea of the different people in his story. All this he has to reveal naturally, not through violent action, but through the ordinary conversations of the main characters.

Ibsen had a remarkable talent for revealing his characters and situations through even the most ordinary scraps of conversation. Notice, for instance, how neatly these few lines show up the difference between the two brothers, the doctor and the burgomaster. Dr. Stockmann is entertaining a few friends to supper, when his brother unexpectedly arrives:

DR. STOCKMANN: Oh, is that you, Peter? Now this is really capital.
BURGOMASTER: Unfortunately, I have only a moment to spare.
DR. STOCKMANN: Nonsense! We shall have some toddy in a minute. You're not forgetting the toddy, Katrina?
MRS. STOCKMANN: Of course not, the water's boiling.
BURGOMASTER: Toddy, too——!
DR. STOCKMANN: Yes; sit down, and make yourself comfortable.
BURGOMASTER: Thanks: I never join in drinking parties.
DR. STOCKMANN: But this isn't a party.
BURGOMASTER: I don't know what else—(*Looks toward the dining room*) It's extraordinary how they can get through all that food.
DR. STOCKMANN: Yes, doesn't it do one good to see young people eat? . .

This gives you a very fair idea of the difference—or one of the differences—between the two men. A little later on, Horster (a sailor) and Billing (a radical journalist) have an equally revealing chat, this time about politics:

MRS. STOCKMANN: And you're going to America?
HORSTER: Yes, that's the intention.
BILLING: But then you'll miss the election of the new Town Council.

HORSTER:	Is there to be an election again?
BILLING:	Didn't you know?
HORSTER:	No, I don't trouble myself about those things.
BILLING:	But I suppose you take an interest in public affairs?
HORSTER:	No, I don't understand anything about them.
BILLING:	All the same, one ought at least to vote.
HORSTER:	Even those who don't understand anything about it?
BILLING:	Understand? Why, what do you mean by that? Society is like a ship; every man must put his hand to the helm.
HORSTER:	That may be all right on shore; but at sea it wouldn't do at all.

Again, the difference in the two men comes out very clearly, but without any forcing of the quiet, natural speech.

What is true of Ibsen's command of dialogue is also true of his handling of the plot. These "problem plays" very often had a tremendous scene, somewhere towards the end, when the characters on opposing sides came face to face. In this play, this happens at a public meeting, and at the end of it the audience is tempted to think that the play is now really over. Nothing could be more wrong. Stockmann has lost his fight; but there is still one act to come, and into it Ibsen brings, not merely all the characters with which the play started, but also new material in the story so that, even at the end, we are learning new things for the first time.

Each of Ibsen's great plays deals with the moment of crisis in the life of the central character. As the play goes on, we are able to piece together the events of the past, and to consider the importance of the new events which are bit by bit introduced. The play is continuously exciting; it begins on the first page, and ends on the last; it is very economical, because it deals with only a small number of characters (though each one is important), and it is compressed into a very short period of time.

The theme of the play

It has been said that the story, or the plot, of a play may take quite a lot of space to explain; but the *theme*—that is to say, what the play is really about—can be stated in a very few words. It is very obvious that Ibsen, in a great number of his plays, was not really concerned with telling a story, unless he was able, at the same time, to say something important about life in general. It should be an easy matter, therefore, to find a "theme" in *An Enemy of the People*.

Dr. Stockmann discovers that the town Baths, which have made a great reputation for their healing properties, are, in effect, poisoned. He is proud of his discovery, and is prepared, with the help of a radical newspaper, to launch the facts upon the unsuspecting townspeople. But the Baths are the town's main source of prosperity, and the cost of improving them would be a crippling charge upon the rates. Stockmann's brother, the burgomaster, is quick to point this out, and the play becomes a battle between the two men. The burgomaster persuades the newspaper to drop the campaign; and the doctor, furious at this, calls a public meeting, convinced that he will show the people the truth. He fails, because the people, the "compact majority" in whose goodness he believes, are not interested in the truth; they are ready to accept any explanation which will not involve them and their town in any unpleasantness. Stockmann is denounced, his job taken away, his name discredited, his family ostracised. At the end of the play, as at the beginning, he makes another "great discovery". "This is what I have discovered, you see; the strongest man in the world is the one who stands most alone."

When you have read this play, you might try putting its theme, its real meaning, into a sentence. You might, of course, find several themes or ideas, all of which are examples of the weakness of human nature. "All men are selfish," you may say—for even the good Dr. Stockmann rather enjoys bringing bad news to the town; or "No man's word is to be trusted"—for it is certainly true that the journalists who were most eager to help Stockmann in his campaign are the very people who turn most viciously against him before the play is over. These statements are, naturally, too vague to be regarded as the real point of the play. However, in Act IV Stockmann says this:

> The majority never has right on its side. Never, I say! That is one of the social lies that a free, thinking man is bound to rebel against. Who make up the majority in any given country? Is it the wise men or the fools? I think we must agree that the fools are in a terrible, overwhelming majority, all the wide world over. But how in the devil's name can it ever be right for the fools to rule over the wise men?

Here we face a real problem. Democracy is based on the idea that all men should share in the affairs of government, and progress is often measured by the extent to which dictatorships are replaced by universally-elected parliaments. Ibsen, furious at the way the "majority" had received his recent plays, seems to be saying exactly the opposite.

Although Dr. Stockmann preaches a fiery sermon in the fourth act of the play, it would hardly be a play at all if it merely preached at us. It does very much more than this: it presents its problem in terms of a mighty conflict—the clash between "principles" and "vested interests", or (to put it another way) between "morality" and "expediency".

Ibsen does something else which is really very important. His characters, although they are simple, are not just pawns, black on one side of the board, white on the other; they are a very varied group of people, and they all have a good deal to do with the way the play evolves.

Story and character

In Act I, Dr. Stockmann is entertaining Billing and Hovstad, both journalists, to supper. Peter Stockmann, his brother, looks in for a moment; then Petra, the doctor's daughter, who has been teaching at night school, brings her father a letter. This confirms his suspicions that the Baths are being poisoned, and the scene ends with Billing and Hovstad agreeing to publish an article by Stockmann in which this scandalous state of affairs is exposed.

Here the plot is slight, but what a deal we learn about the characters. The doctor, a cheerful, ebullient man, childishly proud of his house and its modern gadgets, obviously devoted to his wife and children, is a marked contrast to Peter, who is humourless, pompous, and inclined to be mean. Hovstad, smug and confident; Billing, noisy and excitable; Captain Horster, a sincere man, and a true friend to Stockmann; Mrs. Stockmann and the children, make up the rest of the scene.

Act II introduces us to two more characters: Morten Kijl, the father-in-law of Stockmann, and Aslaksen, the printer. Old Kijl is a cynic; he is convinced that the doctor has some selfish, personal reason for his story of the poison, and he is obviously disinclined to believe a single word of it. Aslaksen, on the other hand, is a "moderate" man, who, though all in favour of publishing the truth, is very anxious to proceed cautiously, not to give offence, and not to hurt anyone's feelings. It is obvious that Aslaksen and Hovstad are not really on the same side, for the one is determined to stir up trouble, the very thing the other wishes to avoid. And trouble there will be, for the Burgomaster threatens Stockmann with dismissal if he does not drop his attacks, and Mrs. Stockmann (up to now a quiet and docile character) speaks up on behalf of her children, and pleads with her husband not to do anything which will harm the family. Stockmann is determined to go on, and in that decision we can already see some of the foolhardiness which is to cause his downfall.

Act III takes place in the printing office. Now we begin to see just how public-spirited the Press really are. Aslaksen is the first to waver: he says, "My heart still belongs to the people; but I don't deny that my reason inclines somewhat towards the authorities—the local ones, I mean." Hovstad is next. Petra, who has been doing some translating for him, attacks him for publishing cheap literature because "That's the very thing the public like." It soon becomes clear that Hovstad is more interested in selling his paper than in exposing scandals; and, to make it worse, it is partly because he is fond of Petra that he is prepared to support her father's cause. Billing backs Aslaksen only because the printer is prepared to finance the paper; but, since Billing is himself hoping to become secretary to the Town Council, his continued support for rebellion can scarcely be guaranteed. So it is, then, that when the Burgomaster arrives at the newspaper office, with a prepared statement about the "rumours" at the Baths, it is *his* article, and not the doctor's, that the paper is prepared to print.

Act IV is the famous meeting. It is held at the house of Captain Horster, the one man who comes out of the whole play with credit. The noisy crowd—including, of course, the inevitable drunk—does not seem to be quite in the mood for a serious discussion on a pressing moral problem. The meeting is a disaster for Stockmann. Aslaksen is elected chairman, and immediately accepts a proposition from the Burgomaster that the lecture from the doctor is unnecessary. Aslaksen and Hovstad both withdraw their support from the doctor; and, when he finally gets up to speak, he decides to attack his audience—the very people whose support he was hoping to gain. Infuriated, they label him an enemy of the people.

Act V begins quietly. Stockmann is collecting the fragments of stone that have been thrown through his windows, and then we learn that the landlord has asked them to quit, that Petra has lost her job, and that Captain Horster has been relieved of his command. The Burgomaster calls, advising his brother to leave the town for a while.

And now, suddenly, the plot takes a surprising twist. It begins when the Burgomaster suggests that his brother, knowing the terms of Morten Kijl's will (by which the bulk of the inheritance goes to Mrs. Stockmann and the children), has deliberately launched his attack upon the town in consultation with his father-in-law. Stockmann is appalled at the suggestion; but his father-in-law enters, and informs him that he has been buying shares in the Baths, and, what is more, using the inheritance money to do it with. The old rogue is still determined that the Baths are pure and clean, and he hopes that, now his own family is threatened, Stockmann will drop his charges. The doctor is still dizzy from this when Aslaksen and Hovstad enter. They have heard that Morten Kijl has been buying shares; they (naturally) assume that Stockmann is in league with him; and they have come back to offer their support—for a little financial consideration. Stockmann's rage is now terrifying, and he practically hurls the newspapermen out of the house. Not only is everybody else selfish and hypocritical, but they are all incapable of believing that anyone could act, as he had done, from disinterested motives. His plans to continue the fight, even to the extent of founding a school, bring the play to an end.

You can see from this summary that each character has his place in the way the play grows and develops. You can see, too, how Ibsen, after the tremendous excitement of the meeting scene, holds in reserve several vital steps in his story so that interest is maintained right to the very end.

Scenes from the play

The two brothers are seen in conflict in the central scene of Act II, beginning at the Burgomaster's line: "Was it necessary to make all these investigations behind my back?"

The whole of Act IV (the meeting scene) is valuable: but, as practice in performing a crowd scene, the beginning—from the opening of the act to the line of Stockmann's "So I am not to be heard?" is particularly suitable.

2. The Devil's Disciple

by BERNARD SHAW

(*This play was first published in 1898, and was afterwards published in a volume which its author entitled* Three Plays for Puritans. *This title is rather an odd one, especially when one considers that the second play in the volume is called* Caesar and Cleopatra. *However, as Shaw explains, he meant these plays to be a complete change from the kind of play that was all too popular in his own time—plays in which highly improbable and sentimental love stories were the chief source of interest.*

The Devil's Disciple *is set in the small town of Websterbridge, New Hampshire, towards the end of the American War of Independence. It is not a piece of history, although one incident, and two of the characters, are taken from real life; it is an exciting story (a "melodrama", Shaw calls it) with plenty of action, plenty of humour, and an assortment of interesting characters. The play has been popular for a very long time. It has been revived frequently in the professional theatre; it has received countless performances by amateur companies; and it made a very successful film.*

Shaw was a great admirer of Ibsen, and he did as much as anyone (except, perhaps, the critic William Archer), to bring Ibsen's plays to English audiences. Not surprisingly, Shaw's first attempts at playwriting were a close imitation of the man he admired so much. They dealt, like those of Ibsen, with serious social problems, and he called them Plays Unpleasant. (*One of them,* Mrs. Warren's Profession, *was regarded as so unpleasant that, for eight years, any public performance of it was forbidden by law. Shaw was furiously angry; and, reading the play today, you might wonder what all the fuss was about.*)

But Shaw was too original a writer to remain under the spell of another man's genius for long. After Plays Unpleasant *came* Plays Pleasant—*a lively and light-hearted group of plays. Shaw had discovered that he had one quality which his Norwegian master lacked—a sense of humour. He realised that he could make people aware of man's frailty and foolishness by making him appear ridiculous.*)

Why a melodrama?

When Shaw called this play "a melodrama" he was referring to its plot. The classic idea of a melodrama contains a heroine (young, beautiful, and virtuous), carried off by the villain (middle-aged, moustachioed, and black-hearted), and rescued in the nick of time by the hero (handsome, brave, and faithful unto death). The classic situation involves the heroine tied to the railway track in the path of an oncoming express; the villain, unaware that he has been discovered, gloating over his triumph; and the hero dashing to the rescue.

In melodrama, all the characters are good or bad, weak or strong, brave or cowardly, and the story is so contrived that, whatever else happens, there is always a race, or a chase, or a breathtaking struggle, to send the audience home excited and satisfied. Melodrama is a kind of escape into a bigger, more colourful, more exciting world; and melodrama continues to be popular, as the success of Hollywood "Westerns" and television "horse opera" clearly shows. When Shaw called *The Devil's Disciple* a melodrama, he simply meant that it had the kind of story which the audiences of the day would recognise and enjoy. Here is his own description of it:

> Every old patron of the Adelphi pit would . . . recognise the reading of the will,ʼ the oppressed orphan finding a protector, the arrest, the heroic sacrifice, the court martial, the scaffold, the reprieve at the last moment, as he recognises beefsteak pudding on the bill of fare at his restaurant. Yet when the play was produced in 1897 in New York . . . the critics, though one said one thing and another another as to the play's merits, yet all agreed that it was novel—*original*, as they put it—to the verge of audacious eccentricity.

The truth is that both Shaw and his critics were perfectly right. The story is a bag of the old familiar tricks; but the character of the hero, and the portraits which Shaw gives us of the other people in the play are all very different from the usual pattern. What is more, it is not just the characters that are unexpected, it is also the dialogue. Shaw at his best is a very witty writer, and this play is full of laughter. Just as Ibsen uses clever dialogue to reveal his characters' true natures, so Shaw uses ridicule to show up the stupid, the pompous, and the selfish.

When two people talk in a Shaw play, one of them nearly always gets the worst of the argument, and, in this way, by making us laugh at the unfortunate person, Shaw also shows that person up in an unfavourable light. When De Stogumber, the English monk in *St. Joan*, declares that "No Englishman is ever fairly beaten", we realise how absurd this is; we laugh at it; and we recognise that, in the character of De Stogumber, Shaw is poking fun at the kind of people who believe that everything their nation does must be perfect. When Judith Anderson, in this play, says of Dick Dudgeon: ". . . He insulted you; he insulted me; he insulted his mother", we smile at her exaggeration, and realise that she is, in fact, rather prim.

Why does Shaw do this? Well, in the first place I think he realised that it does a play no harm to have a good story, and—in this play at least—he went for the kind of story his audiences were used to. Secondly, he had a lot of things to say, and he had a strong suspicion that some of them would shock or offend his audiences; but if he could say them in an amusing and entertaining way, he might persuade the audience to swallow them.

The story of the play

In Act I we meet Mrs. Dudgeon, Christy (her younger son) and Essie, the illegitimate child of Peter Dudgeon, who has just been hanged as a rebel by the English troops at Springtown. Peter is the brother of Timothy Dudgeon, Christy's father, and Christy brings the news that Timothy is also dead, and that the minister is coming round to see Mrs. Dudgeon very shortly. Mr. Anderson, the minister, then arrives, and he is followed by his pretty young wife, Judith, who has come to help Mrs. Dudgeon to prepare the house for the reading of Timothy's will. It appears that Dick Dudgeon (Christy's elder brother, and "the devil's disciple") was at his father's deathbed; and, as all the guests assemble for the reading of the will, Dick bursts into the house. The money has all been left to him; and, at the end of the Act, he chases his mother and the indignant uncles and aunts out of the house with a warning that the English will soon be setting up their rebels' gallows in the market place. Essie, alone, stays with him, and Dick offers to look after her.

Act II moves to the house of the minister. The soldiers are

everywhere, and Judith is afraid. Anderson has asked Dick to call at the house, because he wants to warn him that the soldiers may be looking for him. To Judith's disgust, Dick is invited to take tea with them, but before they can begin, Christy comes to ask Anderson to come to Mrs. Dudgeon, who is very ill. Dick, who has put his coat to dry by the fire, sits down to tea with the minister's wife—an uneasy meal, interrupted this time by the soldiers, who have come to arrest the minister. They naturally assume that the man sitting taking tea is Judith's husband; and Dick, seeing their mistake, takes the minister's old coat from the peg on the door, tells Judith to warn ". . . our friend who was with us just now" of his danger, and goes off under guard. She faints; Anderson returns and, finding her slumped to the floor, jumps to the conclusion that Dick has attacked her. She manages to tell him that Dick has been arrested; but, when he realises that it was a mistake, he grabs his pistols, commandeers a horse, and rides off into the night. Judith assumes that he has gone to save his own skin at the expense of Dick's life.

Act III begins in a waiting room outside the court. Judith, saying she is the wife of the condemned man, has been given a few minutes to speak to him. Dick is quite firm about not revealing his true identity, but he refuses to be called a hero. He doesn't know why he allowed the soldiers to take him, he says, but, as it is too late now to go back on it, he may as well go on pretending to be Anderson. Judith, full of the romantic idea that he did it out of love for her, cannot understand why he is being so noble. However, she obtains permission to be present at the trial, on a promise not to say anything.

We move now into the court, presided over by Major Swindon, and attended by General Burgoyne. He brings news that the rebels (that is, the Americans) have occupied Springtown, and it seems clear that, whatever they plan to do to their prisoner, the war is not going very well for them. The trial then takes place; but, as sentence is passed upon Dick, Judith cannot keep silent any longer, and confesses that he is not her husband. Christy is brought into court to support her statement, but Swindon (who is determined "to make an example of somebody") decides that the execution will take place as planned. The scene ends with further talk between Swindon and Burgoyne, for more disturbing news has reached them. Swindon is in favour of fighting on; Burgoyne, better informed and more realistic, agrees to sign a safe-conduct for someone to come from Springtown to discuss surrender terms with the English forces.

In the market place, just before midday, a large crowd has gathered to watch the hanging. Judith bribes the sergeant to let let her stand near the gallows; the officers arrive, and Dick stands high, with the rope round his neck—when a voice stops the execution, and Minister Anderson rushes into the square, dressed in a captain's uniform, and carrying General Burgoyne's safe-conduct. Anderson has decided that he is better fitted to be a soldier than a parson, and offers to change places—permanently —with Dick. Swindon storms off in a fury, leaving the sergeant to dismiss the men, and Burgoyne—always a gentleman—invites Dick, and Mrs. Anderson, to have lunch with him.

Shaw's diabolical hero

One of Shaw's principal targets in this play was the kind of person whose religion makes him bitter, humourless, bigoted and unreasonable. Mrs. Dudgeon, from all accounts a deeply religious woman, is hard and unsympathetic, and the pious relatives are ridiculous hypocrites. We hear a lot about Dick before he makes his first entrance into the play, and we are prepared for fireworks when he comes in. When he does appear, he is so obviously gay and amusing that we cannot help preferring him to the sober-sided members of his family. We actually like the devil's disciple more than his virtuous relations, which is just what Shaw wants. Here is Dick's arrival, in Act I:

RICHARD: Ladies and gentlemen: your servant, your very humble servant. How happy you all look! How glad to see me! Well, mother; keeping up appearances as usual? that's right, that's right. What! Uncle William! I haven't seen you since you gave up drinking. You *have* given it up, haven't you? Of course you have: quite right; you overdid it. And now, where is that upright horsedealer Uncle Titus? Uncle Titus: come forth. As usual, looking after the ladies!

TITUS: Be ashamed of yourself, sir——

RICHARD: I am: I am; but I am proud of my uncles—proud of all my relatives—who could look at them and not be proud and joyful? Ah, Mr. Anderson, still at the good work, still

> shepherding them. Keep up them to the mark, minister, keep them up to the mark. Come! Clink a glass with me, Pastor, for the sake of old times.
>
> ANDERSON: You know, I think, Mr. Dudgeon, that I do not drink before dinner.
>
> RICHARD: You will, some day, pastor: Uncle William used to drink before breakfast. Come: it will give your sermons unction. But do not begin on my mother's company sherry. I stole some when I was six years old; and I have been a temperate man ever since. So I hear you're married, pastor, and that your wife has a most ungodly allowance of good looks.
>
> ANDERSON: Sir: you are in the presence of my wife.
>
> RICHARD: You servant, madam: no offence. Your deserve your reputation: But I'm sorry to see by your expression that you're a good woman.

We notice from this how little time he has for the funeral faces. Childhood memories of a stern and rigid upbringing have turned him against all that kind of thing. He tells Essie, later in the scene, how he first came to prefer the Devil to God.

> I prayed secretly to him; and he comforted me, and saved me from having my spirit broken in this house of children's tears.

All this talk about worshipping the Devil is really only talk. Dick Dudgeon may have rejected the stern religion of his mother and his straightlaced aunts, but his devilment is only skin deep. Here he is at the minister's house, on his guard against piety, but human and sensible nevertheless. In this little bit of dialogue it is not Dick, this time, who comes off best:

> RICHARD: I come, sir, or your own invitation. You left word that you had something important to tell me.
>
> ANDERSON: I have a warning which it is my duty to give you.
>
> RICHARD: You want to preach to me. Excuse me: I prefer a walk in the rain.
>
> ANDERSON: Don't be alarmed, sir; I am no great preacher. You are quite safe. Mr. Dudgeon: you are in danger in this town.
>
> RICHARD: What danger?
>
> ANDERSON: Your uncle's danger. Major Swindon's gallows.
>
> RICHARD: It is you who are in danger. I warned you——
>
> ANDERSON: Yes, yes, Mr. Dudgeon; but they do not think so in the town. And even if I were in danger, I have duties here which I must not forsake. But you are a free man. Why should you run any risk?
>
> RICHARD: Do you think I should be any great loss, Minister?

ANDERSON: I think that a man's life is worth saving, whoever it belongs to. Come: you'll have a cup of tea, to prevent you catching cold?

RICHARD: I observe that Mrs. Anderson is not so pressing as you are, Pastor.

JUDITH: You are welcome for my husband's sake.

RICHARD: I know I am not welcome for my own, Madam. But I think I will not break bread here; Minister.

ANDERSON: Give me a good reason for that.

RICHARD: Because there is something in you that I respect, and that makes me desire to have you for my enemy.

ANDERSON: That's well said. On those terms, sir, I will accept your enmity or any man's. Judith: Mr. Dudgeon will stay to tea.

If charity and tolerance are Christian virtues, it seems from this that Judith is the odd one out. Later, when Dick takes Anderson's place at the arrest, the poor girl is completely bewildered. It is so unlike the devil's disciple to do a noble thing like that. Then, when her husband deserts Dick (or so she thinks), and she goes to the court to speak to him, she has made up her mind: he did this heroic deed because he was in love with her. But Dick soon puts a stop to her romantic notions:

JUDITH: I disobeyed you. I told him everything. I expected him to come here and save you. I wanted him to come here and save you. But he ran away instead.

RICHARD: Well, that's what I meant him to do. What good would his staying have done? They'd only have hanged us both.

JUDITH: Richard Dudgeon: on your honour, what would you have done in his place?

RICHARD: Exactly what he has done, of course.

It is no use. Judith is like all the young ladies sitting in the theatre to see a play by Bernard Shaw, and Dick has a hard time convincing her that he is unable to explain why he acted as he did. In the end he has to be quite brutal about it, as he says: "I should have done the same for any other man in the town, or any other man's wife. Do you understand that?" But, of course, she doesn't.

You can see by now that the devil's disciple is not such a heathen, after all. He has a lot of good in him; and it seems that Shaw is using him, first to attack the people for whom religion was a terrifying and pleasure-destroying business; and then to attack the silly, romantic notions that all men are either noble heroes or base villains—heroic when inspired by a beautiful woman, and villainous when inspired by anything else. In the third act Shaw turns his fire on stupidity of a different kind. Major Swindon represents the kind of soldier who has got out of the habit of thinking for himself, whereas General Burgoyne is realistic, cynical, and fully aware of the position. This little exchange, at the beginning of the trial, neatly shows us the differences:

BURGOYNE: Any political views, Mr. Anderson?
RICHARD: I understand that is just what we are here to find out.
SWINDON: Do you mean to deny that you are a rebel?
RICHARD: I am an American, sir.
SWINDON: What do you expect me to think of that remark, Mr. Anderson?
RICHARD: I never expect a soldier to think, sir.

Once Richard is off the stage, awaiting execution, it is left to the two officers to discuss the military situation. Now, by making Swindon into a bumbling idiot, and Burgoyne into a disullusioned cynic, Shaw is able to say some biting things about those who give orders, and those who carry them out.

The importance of humour

This play could have been a very solemn affair. After all, although it has a happy ending, the story is serious enough: two deaths before the play begins, and then the reading of a will; an arrest for treason, and another death (Mrs. Dudgeon); a desperately dramatic scene in Anderson's house, followed immediately by the scene before the court; a man sentenced to death; a crowd gathered to watch a public execution. Yet, despite all these fateful events, the play is continuously funny.

Shaw introduces touches of comedy at the most unlikely places. It is Christy, the half-witted brother, who brings the bad news in Act I, and, by his clumsy manner, raises a laugh at the same time. Later in the same scene, Dick's antics at the will-reading turn it into a farcical, rather than a solemn occasion. Act II is more serious, but there is plenty of wit in Dick's conversations with Anderson and Judith, and he manages a joke with the sergeant who comes to make the arrest. We have seen a sample of Dick's mocking speech at his trial; even at the moment of his sentence, he has an amiable argument with Burgoyne as to the relative merits of being hanged or shot. A few moments later, when one of the townsfolk is brought in to identify the prisoner, it is Christy whom the sergeant picks on, and his terror-struck stutterings provide a laugh once again. So throughout the play, Shaw accompanies the action with comedy, as well as using it to ridicule his foolish characters.

There is a very odd thing about plays by Shaw, and this play in particular. Although the play is full of action, and Shaw gives very detailed descriptions of the settings, the characters, and the movements within the play, until you might think that only on the stage are they really successful, the fact is that, because of the humour, and the high quality of the dialogue, the plays are very rewarding to read. Two of the best scenes in this play call for very little movement, and the lines tell us all that we need to know. The first one is the reading of the will, in Act I; the second is the trial scene, which forms the middle part of Act III.

The play also contains several excellent dualogues—that is, scenes in which only two speakers take part. The conversation in Act I between Anderson and Mrs. Dudgeon not only tells us a lot about the play, but also reveals many interesting things about the two characters; then there are the little "tea-table" scene in which Judith is forced to entertain Dick in her husband's absence, the two conversations, in Act III, between Burgoyne and Swindon (one before, one after the trial), and that very difficult, but important scene between Dick and Judith, at the beginning of Act III.

Scenes for detailed study

All the scenes referred to above would make excellent play-reading material, though both the "will" scene and the "trial" scene do gain enormously from being performed. The dualogues, rehearsed a little beforehand, are good practice in showing the attitudes of the two speakers: compare Anderson's tolerance with Mrs. Dudgeon's bitterness; Burgoyne's superiority and contempt with Swindon's mulish lack of imagination, and so on.

If you are looking for scenes to act, and you are prepared to do quite a lot of work on them, then:

(1) *A Crowd Scene.* The whole of the last part of Act III, starting with the entry of the soldiers, and going to the end of the play. You can have as big a crowd, or as many soldiers, as there are people available, and the scene is particularly effective played "in the round"—that is, with the spectators sitting on all four sides of the actors.

(2) *The climax of the whole play*—from the arrival of the soldiers, in Act II, to the end of the act. There are so many changes of mood, so much emotional excitement, that it needs very skilful performing, but it can be very powerful if it is sincerely done.

TERM FOUR

An allegory and a history

The Insect Play by KAREL *and* JOSEPH ČAPEK
Richard of Bordeaux by GORDON DAVIOT

1. The Insect Play

by THE ČAPEK BROTHERS

(Karel Čapek, the great Czech author and principal creator of this famous play, is probably best known in his own country as a writer of short stories, the most famous of which are two volumes called Tales *from* Two Pockets *and* Apocryphal Tales. *Some of these stories retell the famous legends of the past; some are little humorous incidents in the life of the people of Prague, his native city; and one or two are visions of the future, a rather depressing future of war, inhumanity, and destruction.*

Čapek's other famous play is called R.U.R. *or* Rossum's Universal Robots), *and imagines a world where human beings—all but a favoured few—have been reduced to the status of mechanical men, carrying out orders in a blind and mindless way. It is very convenient, and it makes for efficiency, increased production and higher profits—until something goes wrong. The play is a terrible warning to those who would like to turn the world into a huge and soulless factory.*

Karel Čapek died in 1938, as the Nazi forces were preparing to overrun Czechoslovakia. His last plays were grimly prophetic, dealing with the rise of dictatorship, and the struggle of ordinary people to retain their freedom.)

What kind of a play is this?

What I have called *The Insect Play* has been performed under a number of titles. One of the versions is known as *The World We Live In*, and another—perhaps most suitable title—is *And So Ad Infinitum*. This comes from a little verse written by Swift:

> So, Naturalists observe, a flea
> Has smaller fleas that on him prey;
> And these have smaller still to bite 'em,
> And so proceed ad infinitum.

Looking at the list of characters in the play, we observe that they are all, in fact, insects. They are none of them fleas; but, like the parasites in the little verse, they do all prey upon each other. Butterflies quarrel over a love affair, or a piece of poetry, beetles rob each other, ants conduct vast military operations to wipe out tribes of other ants. In this, the smallest part of the animal kingdom, it is a case of "every man for himself". Down there, among the grasses and weeds, in the hollows by the roots of trees, and burrowing into the soil, there is a whole world of creatures, and their behaviour is very much like that of the men and women in "the world we live in".

The idea of animals, birds, and even insects talking to each other is common in children's books, and in fairy stories. Young children are delighted to read about pet animals with real names, and real houses to live in, and charming adventures in a happy animal world, to such an extent that we always associate animal stories with the nursery, or the primary school. But this animal story is not charming, and the adventures of its characters are not really very amusing. This is a serious fairy story, an animal story about thoughtless, cruel, greedy, stupid creatures. We sometimes call this kind of writing an *allegory*.

An allegory is a story in which all the characters represent something different from, and greater than, themselves. In George Orwell's book, *Animal Farm*, the farmyard animals organise a revolt against the farmer, and take over the running of his business; unfortunately, the pigs become the strongest, and they turn the new system into a dictatorship far worse than the old one. In this story, the farmers represent the old aristocratic ruling classes; the animals represent the people who had to work hard for low wages, and are now anxious for a social revolution; and the pigs represent the power-seeking extremists who turn a noble cause into a kind of totalitarian dictatorship.

This is how an allegory works, but it does not always have to be animals or other creatures who play the parts. In Bunyan's *Pilgrim's Progress*, all the characters are human beings, travelling on a long and difficult journey to a distant city. They meet all kinds of problems, as travellers would in the seventeenth century, and not all of them arrive safely. So far, so good; but a glance at the names of the characters and places shows us that this journey is an allegory. The City of Destruction is where all those live who have ceased to care about God; the "problems" that the travellers meet are the temptations, the doubts, and the fears of a Christian life; and the end of the journey is death, and salvation in the world to come.

Look again at the little verse which begins this chapter, and you will see what *The Insect Play* is about. In a world where many people are trying to get as much as they can there is bound to be selfishness, and the insects in this play are made to represent the vice and foolishness of people who have not learned to live at peace with each other.

How does the allegory work in this case? First of all, Čapek has chosen his insects very well. The butterflies represent idle, rich young people, with nothing to occupy their time, and with only one idea in their heads—to trifle with each other, to flirt, to make love, and to be jealous and spiteful at the expense of someone else. Butterflies are beautiful, gay creatures, and their gorgeous colours suggest the rich clothes and expensive jewellery of the rich young people in the play. Butterflies are also very short-lived, and this is paralleled by the characters in the play, whose wild and carefree life does not last long.

The butterflies of the first act are replaced in Act Two by the "Creepers and Crawlers". If the first act is about the world of pleasure, the second is about the world of work. You might expect this to be a busy world, humming with activity as everyone works together to make the world a better place, but it is nothing of the kind. Two beetles have "made their pile"—a heap of useless filth which they trundle aimlessly round with them, until another beetle steals it; two crickets, not long married and expecting their first child, are lucky enough to get a house, but their luck does not last; a fierce ichneumon fly, tirelessly providing for his greedy young, is preying upon every defenceless creature in order to do it.

In the next act we leave the disorganised world of money-grabbers and plunderers, and turn to an organised world—the Ants. These little creatures are famous for the way they work together, and the uncanny understanding which appears to exist in their colonies. Human beings never seem to be as united as this, except when they are engaged upon a military operation. The ants, then, represent the War Machine: men working together, not for the good of the rest of mankind, but in order to destroy their chosen enemies. These ants are Soldier Ants, whose powers of destruction are terrifying.

There are other creatures in the play, apart from the ones which carry the main burden of the story. These, too, have their counterparts in real life, and are introduced into the story to make the "little world" of the insects more complete. There are the moths, who flutter helplessly round the flames, and destroy themselves; there is the parasite; and the chrysalis.

The presentation of the story

The stage is set to represent, greatly magnified, the grasses, and heaps of soil, and tree-roots, of a typical country lane. These things are made to look larger than life so that the actors in their insect costumes will not look out of place. However, in order to introduce us to this strange world, the play provides us with a narrator, much in the same way as Brecht does. We meet him before the curtain rises; he is a ·tramp, and he is talking to a lepidopterist (butterfly-hunter). We have to meet these human characters *in front* of the curtain, or they would look oddly out of proportion against our magnified setting. The lepidopterist tells the tramp something about the habits of butterflies; and, as the tramp settles down to watch them, the curtain opens.

Once the audience has grasped the idea that the tramp is a real person, but the insects are allegorical figures, the playwright has no further problem. The tramp can actually talk to the insects— and frequently does—but, because of the costume, and the fact that he stays outside the picture-frame stage, the audience are quite ready to accept the fact that he is not like them. In this way the play proceeds. Each act has a different set of insect creatures, and each act has its introduction and its commentary.

One of the very best things about plays like this is that the producer, the designer of the settings and costumes, and, in fact, all the people in any way connected with the presentation of the play, are allowed complete freedom to use their imaginations, just as the audience is encouraged to do. Nobody knows anything about this imaginary world, in which strange creatures with insect names talk and behave like men and women; but if the stage directions say: "The scene is an office on the second floor of a large building in London" the audience expects desks, cupboards and filing cabinets, and is grateful for the sound of the lift, or the rumble of traffic outside the window. The office may be dingy or palatial, old-fashioned or ultra-modern, busy or deserted— but it must still, somehow, resemble an office.

No such problem exists with *The Insect Play*. There is, however, an equally serious problem: how can the *presentation* of the play (the décor, costumes, lighting, music, and so on) help the producer and the actors to convey what the author had in mind?

Think first of all about the *setting*. It can obviously be fantastic, colourful, and (naturally) "larger than life". But it should not look like the "woodland glade" in an English pantomime, which usually resembles the painted flowers on the outsides of chocolate boxes. That kind of false prettiness is out of place in a play in which some very sinister things happen. Nor should the setting be all on one level. The ground is naturally uneven, and to a group of small creatures this would seem very much greater than it does to us. What is more, the "busiest" scene of all, the Ant World, will seem much more effective if the ants can be seen marching up and down, on different levels, and in a number of directions. Here again, you see the advantage of this kind of play: while it would be unusual, to say the least, to find a raised platform of a couple of steps in the middle of an office, it is the most natural thing in the world to find the surface of the ground disturbed by hummocks, tufts of grass, clusters of twigs, and stones.

Next, think about the *lighting* of the scene. In our London office, light comes through the window—not directly, but at an angle—and additional light, of a different colour, is provided by the shaded lamp on the typist's desk. The room can go brighter towards noon, or darker towards evening, but there is very little we can do to vary it much more than that. In this play it is a different matter. The light should appear to come from above, and our setting should have its gloomy corners, its odd splashes of sunlight penetrating the leaves or the grasses. The light can change, not merely to suit the time of day, but to suit the scene on the stage. The butterflies are playing about in a warm, rose-pink kind of glow; our beetles live in a yellow and sombre world; for the ants the light is hard and white, and well back on the stage, so that the mechanical figures stand out almost in silhouette against it; and so on. This is not the only way to do it, and you might very well be able to think of other, and better, ways for yourselves; but you can see from this that it is an exciting problem, much more interesting than lighting an office on the stage.

We come now to *costume*. If we were to spend a great deal of money we could do as some science-fiction films do, and disguise our actors so completely that they would look just like insects seen through a powerful microscope. They would look very impressive, no doubt; but can you think of at least two reasons why this is not a good idea?

Well, in the first place these creatures are not simply insects. They are really both insects and human beings at the same time, and the authors of the play are showing us how much the comparison tells us about human behaviour. A real and complete insect costume would make it harder to see this. Secondly, apart from the fact that we would spend our time gazing fascinated at the costume instead of listening to the play, such outfits would make it impossible for us to see the faces of the actors, and so a good deal of their acting would be lost. What we really need is a costume which gives the *idea* of the character, without hampering the actor's movements, or spoiling the effect of what is being said.

Finally, there is room for plenty of *music* in a play like this. Most of us are accustomed to hearing music, in television plays or at the cinema, not merely to begin or end the performance, but also to build up the emotional climaxes. Somehow, it seems quite reasonable to play sinister chords when the murderer is about to strike; stirring, noisy music during a battle; and soft, sentimental melodies as a love-scene develops. In fact, so used to this kind of thing are we that we very often fail to notice it, and it would be hard to imagine a film or television play without this accompaniment. However, what works for the screen does not always work for the stage. Imagine for a moment what the audience would feel like if, in the middle of the "office" play we were discussing earlier, every time the office boy looked across in the direction of the pretty typist, a few bars of sweet music, played by an unseen orchestra, drifted across the stage. It would certainly seem out of place, and it would probably strike everybody as faintly comic.

As long as the play is realistic, music used in this way will seem out of place. But in a *fantasy* like *The Insect Play*, music is one more way, along with costumes, setting, and lighting, of building up the atmosphere. The moths, in the epilogue, actually dance, and they need something to dance to; but in every scene the characters move in special ways—not like office boys, and clients, and managers in an office, but in a way which suggests the kind of people they are. The butterflies dart here and there, excited, changeable, never still for more than a few seconds at a time; the beetles creep, or pounce, or skulk about in fear of their lives; the ants march ruthlessly and mechanically, making everything they do seem inhuman and machine-like; the moths flutter aimlessly and foolishly. The only people who behave normally are the human characters: the tramp, the lepidopterist, the woman and the woodcutter. And remember, they are not really inside the play; they are just part of the chorus.

Several stories inside one

At the beginning of this play the tramp sits down to rest; at the end of the play he dies. This is the story outside the play, but it is too simple to make a play by itself. Before he dies he talks to the lepidopterist, and at the end of the play the woodcutter and the woman find the body. This is the *framework* of the play, and all this takes place in front of the stage. The main action is, however, not one story, but several. The tramp, resting by the roadside, glimpses the lives of different kinds of creatures, and each of these glimpses is complete in itself. The butterflies do not appear again after the first scene, and similarly we see no more of the beetles when their scene is finished. The third and last scene, the tremendous war between the two tribes of ants, is also complete; then, as the tramp begins to die, he hears (as in delirium) a few voices from the earlier scenes. The moths fly around for a few seconds; two snails find his body, and pass on.

In talking about this play I have not told you the actual story of any of these scenes. In a way, they are not stories, but incidents. They give us the impression that life will always go on like this, and it does not have a neat beginning, middle, or end. Foolish, rich young people will go on flirting, and wasting their precious time; men and women will go on fighting for survival, quite selfish and intolerant towards those in the same position as themselves; there will always be war. So the world goes on . . . and so *ad infinitum*.

The text for the stage

This play has been translated from the original Czech by Paul Selver, and when the play was first performed in London in 1932 it was this translation which was available, and no other. However, if you look at the play as it appears in anthologies, you will see at once how difficult it is to act. There are many long speeches and it seems at times as though the tramp is preaching to the audience, and not actually telling the story at all. What might very well have worked very successfully in Europe in the 1920s seems very much out of place to us here and now; and even in 1923 it seemed very strange. As a result, two English writers, Nigel Playfair and Clifford Bax, men with a great deal of experience of the theatre, took the Paul Selver translation and adapted it for the stage. They reduced many of the long speeches; they made the dialogue much more natural; they shortened the play considerably, without losing any of the point of each scene; and they rewrote some of the tramp's monologues into simple verse. The result was a very successful text.

Here are one or two examples of the neat and effective way this stage version scores its points. Here, first of all from Act One, is the old familiar situation: a wise, "experienced" lover, a foolish, romantic young man, and a flighty girl are talking about the only subject that interests them:

IRIS: . . . Tell me, my precious, don't women really interest you any longer?

FELIX: No—I'm weary of them.

IRIS: Oh, you men—you're such cynics. You have your fun—as much fun as you can get—and then you say "I'm weary of them." It's a terrible thing to be a woman.

VICTOR: Why?

IRIS: We never grow tired of love. Have you had a terrible past, Felix? When did you first fall in love?

FELIX: I don't know. I forget. It was so long ago. I was a schoolboy.

VICTOR: Ah, you were still a caterpillar. Gobbling up all the leaves.

IRIS: A little kitty kitty kitty caterpillar. Was she dark and beautiful?

FELIX: As beautiful——

IRIS: As what?

FELIX: As beautiful as you.

IRIS: And did she love you?
FELIX: I don't know. I never spoke to her.
IRIS: Good heavens! What did you do to her then?
FELIX: I looked at her from afar.
VICTOR: Sitting on a green leaf?
FELIX: And wrote poems, letters—my first novel.
VICTOR: It's appalling what a lot of leaves a caterpillar uses up.

We can just hear Felix, defiantly trying to sound grown up, and the smooth Victor cheerfully making fun of him, while Iris encourages him to make a fool of himself.

Now, compare this casual, lighthearted dialogue with the staccato speeches of the ants. They worship the State, and in their world everything that exists must work to serve the State. The doctrine is a reasonable one, provided that humanity and tolerance are not forgotten; but to the ants of this play, the State must be served mechanically, ruthlessly, and without regard for personal feelings. Their minds are like machines, and their talk is appropriately slick, quick, and rhythmical:

ENGINEER 2:   We are surrounded by enemies.
CHIEF ENGINEER: We defeated the Black Ants——
ENGINEER 2:   And starved out the Browns——
CHIEF ENG: And subjugated the Greys, and only the Yellows are left; We must starve out the Yellows—
ENG. 2:   We must starve them all out.
TRAMP: Why?
CHIEF ENG.:   In the interests of the whole.
ENG. 2:   The interests of the whole are the highest.
CHIEF ENG.:   Interests of race—
ENG. 2:   Industrial interests—
CHIEF ENG.:   Colonial interests—
ENG. 2:   World interests—
CHIEF ENG.:   Interests of the world.
ENG. 2:   Yes, yes, that's it.
CHIEF ENG: All interests are the whole's.
ENG. 2:   Nobody may have interests but the whole.
CHIEF ENG.:   Interests preserve the whole.
ENG. 2:   And wars nourish it.
TRAMP: Ah, you're warlike ants.
ENG. 2:   He knows nothing.

You can see how inhuman all this is. You will have noticed, too, that the ants do not think what they are saying, but just speak in slogans, as if they had swallowed all the propaganda without even bothering to see if it made sense. Politicians have a habit of giving their supporters neat little phrases to hang on to, and some of the more successful ones find their way on to posters, into newspapers, and across the country in public meetings and political party broadcasts. After a time they become so familiar that people begin to accept them as true, without criticism and without question. These ants have been, as the saying goes, "indoctrinated"—and now they believe, blindly, stupidly, and completely. They no longer think for themselves.

A mirror or a pulpit?

Many people, when they come across a play like this one, protest that it is really a sermon; that the author, forgetting that it is the first duty of a play to entertain, is using the theatre as a means of putting over his own social, political, or religious ideas. This is quite often a fair and reasonable criticism, but I doubt whether it is specially true of *The Insect Play*. Despite its serious theme, this play is extremely entertaining. As we watch it, we are not merely amused by the comedy of the absurd insects who inhabit its scenes, we are also captivated by the novelty of the setting. We recognise the truth in many of its observations about life, and we are interested in what is going to happen to the characters.

So much for the play as entertainment. But is it, also, propaganda? I do not think so. It certainly criticises the way people behave, and it makes humanity out to be a very frail and fallible thing; but it does not put forward a ready-made solution to our problems. It shows up men's faults, and it naturally assumes that men would be better without them, but it does it in such a way that we enjoy the play while we are watching it, and—perhaps days or weeks after the performance—we remember some of the wise things it said.

Scenes from the play

Each of the separate "acts" of this play stands by itself, and so it is possible to consider each one as a kind of one-act play, suitable for study or performance away from the play as a whole. Particularly useful, and effective, are:

(1) The first part of "Creepers and Crawlers" (Act II). Here the actor needs to imitate, in voice and gesture, the stupid, greedy, and vulgar people represented by the flies and beetles of the play. There are plenty of real-life models on which to base this scene, but it is important to remember that the characters are *caricatures*, and should be played accordingly.

(2) The whole of "The Ants" (Act III)—and especially the later part of the scene—is valuable. Much of the effect here is got by the sharp, mechanical ryhthm of the speakers, and the marching movements of the minor characters. Towards the end of the scene, the whole thing works up to an exciting climax, in which all the players, whether they have important lines to say or not, play a vital part.

2. Richard of Bordeaux

by GORDON DAVIOT

(This is really a "chronicle play"—which means that it tells the main events in the life of Richard II, in the order in which they happened. The plot and the characters are taken from the history of England in the fourteenth century; only the actual words spoken are invented by the playwright. The play has twelve scenes, and contains a large number of characters; the action spreads across England, into France and North Wales, and it covers a period of almost thirteen years.

History plays have always been popular. Shakespeare wrote more than a dozen, and in this he was only following the example of others—Marlowe, for instance—who had preceded him. Throughout the seventeenth and eighteenth centuries, large-scale tragedies based on the lives of famous historical figures continued to be written; and, in our own time, we can find examples of plays about Queen Elizabeth, Martin Luther, Simon Bolivar, Galileo, Sir Thomas More, and many others.

History (provided that we do not have to mug it up for examinations) has a fascination for most of us. We are always interested to find out what life was like for those who lived in the past. For this reason, historical novels, as well as plays, will always find a public. It is interesting, in this connexion, to note that "Gordon Daviot" is the penname of novelist Josephine Tey, whose novel, Daughter of Time, *deals with the life of another English king, Richard III.)*

Finding our way about

If the curtain rises on a modern play, we usually have a very fair idea of what kind of place we are looking at, and what kind of people are involved in the action. If we wait patiently for a few minutes, they will tell us enough about themselves to enable us to work out the rest for ourselves. We recognise the clothes they wear, the jobs they do, the problems they have; and, when they open the door and go out into the street, we can easily imagine what they will find there.

A history play does not work like this. Most people who have bought tickets for *Richard of Bordeaux* know very little about fourteenth-century England, and they rely on the playwright to keep them informed. They may dimly realise that, in those days, parliament had less power, and rulers more, than they have today; they may also know that "a friend at court"—meaning someone, usually titled, to whom the king gave a sympathetic ear —was a very useful friend to have. But they almost certainly know nothing of the men who lay behind the whispered plots and political intrigues of the time. So the first job of the playwright is to see that, as each scene comes along, the audience do not merely understand the dialogue, but they also appreciate the situation.

The playwright's next problem is one of *selection*. A king is faced, every day, with new meetings and new decisions, and a whole host of soldiers, advisers, ambassadors and servants pass across his life. No play can cope with all of them, and it is for the writer to decide which to leave out. The interesting question is: how does he decide?

If you look at this play carefully, you will notice a strange thing. Richard was extravagant, fond of tournaments and hunting, and splendid state occasions; yet in every scene we see him accompanied by small groups of people. There are no court levées, no battle scenes, no royal processions—nothing but affairs of state, private conversations, and moments of relaxation. Gordon Daviot refers often to the public side of the king's behaviour, but it looks very much as if she is mainly interested in Richard as a *person*, not simply as a king. We hear about the cheering crowds, the royal wedding, the armies gathering to support one side or another, but we have to see them only in our imagination.

The play appears to have been written to show us what kind of man Richard was. He is a very interesting king, because he has many sides to his character, and this play reveals him in all his different moods. But a string of scenes, each one telling us something more about one man, is hardly good enough to make a play. We know very well that a play depends on more than just character; it needs conflict, a theme, a progress towards a climax. This is no problem for Gordon Daviot. Richard's life as king was spent in a series of struggles with the noble lords whose chosen policy it was to guide the fortunes of England. Sometimes Richard wins, sometimes he loses, and at all times he is involved in a hectic diplomatic game. We follow his fortunes: each scene advances the struggle one more stage, and each scene shows us something fresh about the hero of the play. What is more, each scene fills in for us a little of the background of the times, so that even those of us who know no history can understand the situations in which the king finds himself.

The events of the play

So many things happen in *Richard of Bordeaux* that it might be useful to give here a brief summary of the main points:

ACT I

Scene 1: Two page-boys are gaming in a room in the palace. Richard storms out of a council meeting, furious at the way he is being treated. The trouble seems to be over France. Anne, Richard's wife, appears, and urges him to be patient.

Scene 2: Back in the council chamber; Gloucester and Arundel are urging Richard to war with France; Richard wants to make a peaceful settlement, and he is supported by the Chancellor (De La Pole), Burley, and his close friend, Robert De Vere, Earl of Oxford. Lancaster and York try, without success, to settle the quarrel.

Scene 3: We meet Henry (son of Lancaster, later Henry IV) and his wife. The scene shows us the contrast between the warlike Henry and the artistic, peaceful Richard. Thomas Mowbray, a friend of the king, announces his intention of marrying Arundel's daughter. This amounts to "going over to the other side"—as Richard realises.

Scene 4: A year later. Robert de Vere is now Duke of Ireland. Gloucester and Arundel head a deputation to Richard. They bring a refusal from the House of Commons to grant further money to the king, and they declare their intention of accusing Richard's friends of treason. They plan to remove from office all those who opposed them in the council on the question of war with France. As a result, De La Pole, Burley, and others are impeached or dismissed.

Scene 5: Richard, furious at the way he has been treated, has rallied his friends to fight the combined soldiers of Gloucester, Mowbray, and Henry. It is a month later than the previous scene: news comes that Richard's supporters were routed at Radcot Bridge, and that Robert De Vere ran away. De Vere arrives, and Richard accuses him of cowardice.

ACT II

Scene 1: Three years later. The king, now 23 years old, asserts his authority. He summons Gloucester and Arundel, and demands the resignation of their supporters. He has made his peace with Mowbray (by offering him a gift of land); he has invited Lancaster—back from an expedition to Spain—to join his council. As the scene ends, Anne, the queen, contracts the plague.

Scene 2: Two years later, Richard, back from a "goodwill mission" to Ireland, decides to settle the French question finally by marrying the daughter of the French king—a child of eight. Gloucester, naturally, protests; Richard drops Mowbray a hint that he might take Gloucester with him on a visit to France and thence "dispose" of him.

Scene 3: A short street scene, in which we gather from the gossip that both Gloucester and Arundel have been dealt with.

Scene 4: During a banquet, Henry and Mowbray quarrel. They agree to fight, but Lancaster intervenes on his son's behalf. Richard therefore agrees to exile them, Henry for six years, Mowbray for life. The quarrel was an excellent excuse for Richard to get Mowbray out of the way, now that he had served his purpose.

Scene 5: Three years later. Paris. Henry, in exile, is visited by the Archbishop of Canterbury, with the news that Lancaster is dead, and that Henry is therefore entitled to his father's estates. However, it seems that Richard, in order to conduct a military campaign in Ireland, has helped himself to Lancaster's property. Canterbury has with him a long list of names of those who would support Henry if he returned to England to claim his title. He decides to do so.

Scene 6: Conway Castle. Richard has returned from Ireland, but his attempts to raise troops have failed—they are all flocking to Henry's banners. Richard is taken to London, under escort.

Scene 7: Henry offers Richard "safety" in return for his abdication. Richard agrees; Henry immediately orders him to be "escorted" to Pomfret Castle. Richard despatches his faithful secretary, Maudelyn, to look after the queen at Windsor; and he prepares to leave London for the last time.

This long catalogue of facts may seem rather too much for one play, but if we look again at the two acts we can see clearly how the play hangs together. Act I shows us a young and inexperienced king, full of ideals about peace with France, and fighting a losing battle against the determined opposition of his uncle, Gloucester. We see Richard foolishly spending money, tactlessly giving good jobs to his personal friends, treating parliament with contempt—and, at the end of the first act, paying for his foolishness by being forced to bow to his uncle's wishes. During this act, Daviot carefully introduces Henry—very early in the play—and shows him to be just the opposite of Richard: he cares more for good weapons than for fine clothes; he is not artistic, lighthearted, or playful—to him life is a serious matter—but he is strong, dependable, and manly.

In the second act, Richard starts off at the peak of his good fortune. Now of age, he deals with his enemies, and handles parliament with a confidence and assurance which he did not previously possess. He has settled the Irish question; made peace with France; silenced Gloucester and Arundel; and, by a lucky accident, put Mowbray and Henry out of harm's way. Then, suddenly, he makes the one foolish mistake which costs him his crown (and, later, his life). Still extravagant, still gambling with the popularity which he has never really had, he finds himself alone, without friends, without an army, and with the services of only one or two faithful companions to see him through. He has had his chance to rule England successfully, and he has thrown it away.

As you see, there is a pattern in all these events. Richard appears in almost every scene, and each time he appears we learn something new about him. In addition, we are constantly

reminded of three or four basically important ideas which seem
to control the action of the play. Let us consider some of them.

The themes behind the action

Certain facts about Richard's character constantly crop up.
He is a very extravagant man, and he frequently antagonises
parliament—and the nobles—by his wasteful spending. This is
not merely mentioned many times; it is actually *used*, very
skilfully, to help us to follow the fortunes of the king. Notice, in
Act I, Scene 1, he talks to the page-boys who are gambling;
notice, too, in scene 3, how his love of finery is contrasted to
Henry's soldierly plainness. Notice how his first expedition to
Ireland is made an excuse for lavish entertainment; and, finally,
notice how—as his fortunes ebb away—he has no fine clothes to
pack in Conway Castle, and not even a decent pair of shoes when
he is to leave the Tower for Pontefract.

Another idea which is common to many scenes is the devotion
of Richard's closest friends. His great affection for Robert De
Vere, Earl of Oxford, runs through the play: he listens to his
opinion in everything; he cannot bear to meet him when Robert
has run away from the fighting; and, long after he has dropped
out of the play, Richard remembers him, and refers to his old
friend. Conversely, this friendship was not one-sided. Burley
and De La Pole risked treason charges rather than desert Richard;
Tressilian stays loyal long after all hope of raising an army has
gone; and the former page (later secretary) Maudelyn is ready
to follow the king to the death, if need be. Richard understood
the depth of these men's affection, and he never let them down.
The only "friend" he betrayed was Mowbray; but Mowbray's
friendship was a matter of convenience rather than love.

It seems curiously ironic that Richard, who had such deep
concern for the ordinary people of England, should have been
overthrown simply because the people preferred someone else.
In this play, we never meet the common folk at all (except in one
very short, and rather unnecessary scene). However, the wishes
of "the people" are constantly being discussed. And, linked to
the idea of popularity is the idea of war with France. England's
prestige at this time was measured by her success in subduing the
French, and the question of peace or war with France runs

through practically every scene of the play. To some, the Black Prince was a national hero, and his example should be followed; to others (Richard included), an honourable settlement was better than a wasteful and futile military campaign. Richard chose the unpopular view, and it is probable that he would have been better supported against Henry if he had not done so.

In three or four quiet, short scenes we are shown the love and trust that existed between Richard and Anne, his queen. She is ready to comfort and sustain him; to speak for him to his opponents; she accepts him, with all his faults, all his moods, and all his misfortunes. After her death, he wants to pull down the palace where they had lived together so happily, and her memory is always fresh in his mind.

The style of the play

Sometimes, and particularly in certain types of historical novel, the characters have a quaint habit of speaking. They utter exclamations like "Gadzooks!" and "By my halidom!" They use "thee" and "thou" quite indiscriminately, and they distort the English language in order to give the reader the impression that everything in the story happened a long time ago. There is none of this foolishness in *Richard of Bordeaux*. Gordon Daviot has wisely (but for one tiny scene) confined her characters to people with education and social position, and so we are not surprised to find them speaking clear, good, and fluent English. Of course, they do not use modern slang, or colloquialisms which we would recognise immediately as belonging to the twentieth century; on the other hand, they speak in a clear, straightforward manner, and when we hear them, and see the costume they wear in the setting of the play, we find no difficulty in accepting the fact that we are watching a piece of fourteenth-century life.

Gordon Daviot does not, in fact, use tricks of language in order to get her dramatic effects, nor does she use the same theatrical device more than once. The discovery that Anne has caught the plague is placed at the end of a scene in which Richard is delighted at getting all his own way, and so the contrast here is very effective. We are not surprised; but the effect of the tragic happening on the king, coming so soon after his triumph over Gloucester, is very striking. Another effective "curtain-scene" is the one in which Richard has just banished Mowbray and Henry. Mowbray (over-confident as ever) stays behind to speak to Richard, convinced that his banishment was merely a trick to pacify the others; when he discovers that Richard is in earnest, he is thunderstruck.

Not all the scenes end on a moment of high drama. Some of the best scenes end very quietly. Several of them, especially those in which Richard, in Act I, is having trouble with the Council, end with a comforting word from Anne, or one of his close friends; and the very last scene of all, when Richard is about to leave London for the last time, is almost entirely made up of a moving conversation between Maudelyn and the king. But not entirely so; the end of the scene is a mocking reminder of the king's long and futile struggle with the Commons:

RICHARD: Goodbye, Maudelyn. I shall remember the shoes; and the
            night you came to light candles. You have been a good,
            friend to me. (*Someone calls outside*) They are very impatient
            with all time in front of them.
MAUDELYN: Yes, they have to meet a committee of the Commons. One
            of the guard told me.
RICHARD: Oh? Are the Commons going to vote Henry a fortune in
            consideration of his services to the country?
MAUDELYN: No, sir. The gifts he made to his followers were out of all
            reason, they say. They are complaining of his extrava-
            gance.
RICHARD: Extravagance! Isn't life amusing? (*There is an impatient
            knocking*) Goodbye, Maudelyn. (MAUDELYN *kisses his hand
            fervently and almost runs out*) Extravagance! How Robert
            would have laughed!

There are many scenes as quiet and moving as this one, but the great quality of this play lies in its arguments. When Gloucester and the king are at each other over the matter of France, when men are attacking each other's beliefs, when there is a fine set-to in the council chamber or the court, then history comes to life. Even when Anne talks to Mary (Henry's wife) we can feel the smouldering disagreement. Robert De Vere, Earl of Oxford, is seen talking to one of the ladies-in-waiting; notice how neatly the writing shows up the foolishness of Mary, and the common sense and sympathy of Anne:

MARY: Is it true, madam, what they say?

ANNE: It hardly ever is. But what do you mean particularly?

MARY: Well, it may be indiscreet of me, but they say that Lord Oxford finds your waiting-woman very attractive.

ANNE: Agnes is very attractive.

MARY: Her manners are very foreign.

ANNE: She has been brought up, like me, in a country where women do not wait until they are spoken to before they speak.

MARY: It must be so distressing for his poor wife when people tell her.

ANNE: Then why do they tell her?

MARY: It is only right that she should know what is going on.

ANNE: What is going on?

MARY: Oh, well, madam, you know best, of course.

Finally, here is a little of one of those disputes about France which run through the whole play. Richard, in the first scene of the play, has walked out of the Council; now, as Arundel is bursting with rage, and practically accusing the king of treason, Richard returns:

RICHARD: You were saying, Lord Arundel . . .?

ARUNDEL: I was protesting yet once more, sir, against this monstrous suggestion of—of—

RICHARD: Of peace.

ARUNDEL: Yes, of peace. England is not beaten, sir. She has had reverses, of course, but so has France. The spirit of the people is not broken, sir; the will to win is still there and we have a first-rate army. Once this armistice ends, there is nothing to hinder us from making a new invasion which will result in unqualified victory, a complete vindication of our policy, and a still greater glory for England.

RICHARD: And more cripples begging in the gutters, and more taxes to cover the cost!

ARUNDEL: You can have no war without wastage, sir. As to the cost, the captured provinces in France will more than repay the costs—

RICHARD: When they are captured.

ARUNDEL: And I cannot help saying, sir, that it is a poor day for England when she has to count the cost before she takes her stand in a rightful war.

RICHARD: Oh, let us have done with humbug! My grandfather invaded France in a trumped-up cause which even he himself didn't believe in. My father helped him because he liked the game. They both lost practically all they had gained before they died; and now you suggest that I should lay waste France and kill forty thousand men because it is my sacred duty.

There is something very modern about this. It is easy, as Arundel does, to ignore the realities and to talk in empty phrases about "honour" and "duty". It is left to Lancaster, the shrewd and experienced statesman, to ask the vital question:

> LANCASTER: But—supposing for a moment that this peace policy of yours is carried into effect, can you guarantee that France will be equally conscious of her high mission in European politics? Once our army is disbanded, how can you trust them to refrain from snapping up such a juicy morsel as England will be?
>
> RICHARD: Because France wants peace, too, in her heart. There is no peace, because France too is plagued by people like you, like the Commons, like Arundel, like Gloucester, who say: "It would be shameful to stop! We must go on."
>
> ARUNDEL: And we must! I am not ashamed to say it . . .

Political problems do not seem to have changed much since 1385 —why, then, should the language be different?

The other Richard II

It is really remarkable how different two plays on the same subject can be. Shakespeare's *Richard II* is an excellent example of this difference. Whereas Gordon Daviot's play starts back in 1385, Shakespeare begins with the quarrel between Mowbray and Henry, nearly ten years later. In other words, Shakespeare's first scene corresponds to Act II, Scene 4 of the modern play. While Gordon Daviot gives us the whole narrative of Richard's life from the days when the kingdom was virtually controlled by his uncles, Shakespeare builds all the action round the dismissal of Henry; his father's death; the return of Henry from France; the deposition of the king, his arrest, and his death in Pomfret Castle.

This makes a surprising difference to the way history is presented. In *Richard of Bordeaux* the audience is informed about the main events as they happen; but in *Richard II* Gloucester is already dead, Robert De Vere has been replaced by other "favourites", Anne is dead, the quarrels over France have been settled—at least for the time being—and we must pick up all this information as the play goes along.

Another very important difference between the two plays is in the way the vital scenes are presented. Gordon Daviot, as we have noticed, allows little pomp and ceremony to enter her play, but Shakespeare revels in it. Thus, the two accusers (Mowbray and Henry) confront each other in the open court; a little later on, they meet to fight a duel at Coventry, surrounded once again by their glittering supporters, and the fight is stopped at the last minute by Richard, who banishes them both instead. Shakespeare shows us the death of John of Gaunt, Duke of Lancaster—a tremendous scene, with the king present; he also shows us the meeting between Richard and Henry, the one returned from Ireland, the other from France, as they confront each other with their supporting soldiers drawn up behind them.

Shakespeare can do this for two reasons: first, because he used an open stage, with little or no scenery, and crowd scenes were easy to manage; and second, because, having decided to concentrate his play on a comparatively short period of time, he could afford to spread himself in these large and impressive scenes.

Both plays, however, avoid contact with the ordinary people of England. *Richard of Bordeaux*, as we have seen, has one short scene in which a group of people discuss the "disappearance" of Gloucester, but the scene is not very interesting, and adds nothing to the play. Shakespeare, on the other hand, towards the end of *Richard II*, introduces two gardeners, who in their simple way compare the proper government of the country with the proper care of a garden. This is a telling scene; it comes at the point where Richard is losing his power to Henry, and it suggests, in very simple language, some of the reasons why Richard has been a failure as a king.

Scenes and characters

Apart from Richard himself, the characters in this play are fairly simple, and most of the scenes—whether read or acted—have plenty of dramatic contrast. One of the most interesting scenes to work on would be:

> ACT II, SCENE 1. It begins with the angry Gloucester and Arundel, kept waiting by the king; it contains two surprises —the return of Mowbray and Lancaster, and the triumph of Richard over his uncle; and it has the sudden, tragic twist at the end, as Anne is confirmed as a plague victim.

The other effective scene, though in quite a different way, is the "party" scene (ACT I, SCENE 3)—effective because, underneath the small-talk and gossip, we feel the tensions: Richard's dislike of Henry, the sharp differences in their characters, the unfortunate marriage of Mowbray, the lack of sympathy between Anne and Mary, Henry's wife. It is a good scene to act, because it has a sense of free-and-easy movement, relaxed conversation, food and wine—and yet the little moments of uneasiness are all there, too.

TERM FIVE
Two comedies

The Taming of the Shrew by WILLIAM SHAKESPEARE
The Playboy of the Western World by J. M. SYNGE

1. The Taming of the Shrew

by WILLIAM SHAKESPEARE

(This is one of Shakespeare's early plays, and is an amusing mixture of farce and romantic comedy. The plot—like the plot of nearly every Shakespeare play—is not at all original; the story is an old one, but the language and the characters are all Shakespeare's. In fact, there are two stories here, running parallel, something we find very commonly in comedy, both in Shakespeare and elsewhere. However, the two stories are linked together, and some characters take part in both.

We can call the play a "farce" because it depends for some of its laughs on disguises, misunderstandings, and scenes of knockabout or "slapstick"; on the other hand, part of the play is concerned with courtship, and the fortunes of the lovers give the play its title to "romantic comedy". The whole play is sunny and light-hearted, packed with amusing situations, and well-contrasted characters. The language is straightforward and vigorous, the action swift and varied. Although it is set in Renaissance Italy, it is not a "period piece"—any kind of costume will do, and any setting is appropriate, provided that the climate is sunny and warm—for the jokes are as fresh now as they were when the play was first written.

Too many people are inclined to treat a Shakespeare play as a philosophical document, instead of something to be enjoyed in the theatre. Certainly there is effective satire in Twelfth Night, *and serious reflection on human behaviour in* The Tempest; *but don't let us forget that* The Taming of the Shrew *is "for amusement only".)*

A play within a play

We saw this arrangement once before—in *The Insect Play*—where one character (the Tramp) was the onlooker at the antics of the various insect characters who made up the main part of the story. In this play, the same sort of thing happens.

A drunken down-and-out, Christopher Sly, is found lying on the ground by some young men, servants to a nobleman who lives in the vicinity. Sly is so overcome with drink that he does not realise where he is, or what he is doing, and so it occurs to the young men that they might take him to their master's house and make game of him. When Sly recovers his wits, he is in a fine bed, in a large room of a country mansion, being waited on by a number of attentive servants. They pretend that he is wealthy, and that all the riches of the house belong to him; what is more, they tell him that a play is to be performed that day, in his honour. Whereupon the members of the household improvise a stage, some properties and furniture, and the play, *The Taming of the Shrew*, is performed. After the performance (which Sly watches from his bed, interrupting occasionally), he finds himself once more back in the gutter.

These scenes with Sly have nothing at all to do with the play itself, and so they are very often omitted in performance. Not every theatre is so designed that it can accommodate a bed on the front of the stage without spoiling the audience's view of the actual play; and not every theatre company has enough actors—even allowing for the fact that the "servants" would, some of them, take part in the play—to present the play and the extra scenes successfully. In Shakespeare's own theatre it was no problem. The stage platform was very wide, with the audience sitting or standing on three sides of it, and the actors moved about freely, so that none of them were out of sight for very long. It was also common practice in Elizabethan theatres for spectators (those who could afford to pay extra) to sit on stools on the stage itself, without seriously interfering with the performance. This custom was not very popular with the actors, but they had to make the best of it. An interesting further point is this: there are very few lines for the drunken Sly to speak during the actual performance of *The Taming of the Shrew*, and it therefore seems likely that the part was given to a clown who would make comments of his own, to the actors and to the audience, and who would even, at times, get up from his bed and get himself mixed up in the action of the play. It seems extremely unlikely that Shakespeare would go to the trouble to invent this character for the sake of two pages at the beginning of the play, and a few lines at the end.

Shakespeare, an actor himself, might have introduced Sly in order to poke fun at the practice of allowing people to sit so close to the players. In a later play, *The Knight of the Burning Pestle* by Francis Beaumont and John Fletcher, two playgoers, a tradesman and his wife, not only buy stools on the stage; they talk all the time, interrupt the action, and even persuade the actors to allow their apprentice, Ralph, to take part in the performance

The plot of the play

Forgetting about Christopher Sly for the moment, let us look at the main story of the play. The action is very complicated, since at least five of the characters pretend to be someone else during the course of the play; and, to make it worse, the Italian names are sufficiently alike to be easily confused. It might, therefore, be simpler to disentangle the characters, and to give an idea of the two stories, without bothering too much about the precise order in which things happen. In any case, everything is quite clear if we can *see* the play as well as read it.

Baptista is a wealthy merchant of Padua, and he has two daughters. The young one, Bianca, is beautiful, and modest, and charming; the elder one, Katarina, is violent, bad-tempered, and, in fact, "a shrew". There are two men in love with Bianca—Hortensio, a neighbour, and an old man, Gremio. They are both anxious for permission to court Bianca, but her father, who sees himself being left with Katarina on his hands, imposes a crafty condition: he is resolved

> . . . not to bestow my youngest daughter
> Until I have a husband for the elder.

A third suitor, Lucentio, a travelling student (accompanied by his two servants, Tranio and Biondello) sees Bianca, and immediately falls in love with her. But what is to be done about the condition? None of them wants anything to do with Katarina, and her father is determined that she shall be the first to be married.

At this point, Petruchio, an old friend of Hortensio, comes on the scene. (He has an idiotic servant, Grumio, who follows him

PIA

everywhere.) He hears the story of Baptista's two daughters, and is quite ready—for a little financial assistance, of course—to woo Katarina, thus leaving the others free to try their luck with Bianca. And now the two "stories" begin to follow their separate courses.

Baptista wants teachers to instruct his daughters, and both Lucentio and Hortensio have the same idea. Lucentio has already given Tranio his cloak, and presented him to Baptista as the real Lucentio, so that he himself can, disguised, obtain employment as a teacher in Baptista's house. At the same time, Hortensio disguises himself as a music-teacher, and gets into Baptista's house also. These two, Licio (Hortensio) and Cambio (Lucentio) offer their love to Bianca while pretending to be instructing her. She prefers Lucentio, and poor Hortensio realises that he is beaten. He resolves to marry "a wealthy widow", and retires from the fight.

Meanwhile, Tranio has applied for permission to woo Bianca, and so has old Gremio. (Tranio is only acting on his master's behalf, but Baptista does not know this.) Baptista is prepared to listen to these candidates only when Katarina is taken care of; whereupon Petruchio meets the girl, has a stormy interview with her, declares his intention of marrying her the following Sunday, and obtains her father's consent in spite of her vigorous protests. Petruchio carries off Katarina, as he promised—in fact, he appears on the wedding day dressed in rags, upsets the marriage service, insults the priest, invites all and sundry to the feast, and then disappears with Katarina before the party has even started. This is his first act in his declared policy of "taming" the shrew.

With Katarina safely married, Baptista is prepared to let Bianca go to the highest bidder. Tranio (still speaking for his master, Lucentio) and old Gremio are asked to declare the size of their fortunes. Tranio wins; but is a little put out when Gremio suggests that he has produced no proof that the money will come to him when his father dies. Tranio is, for a few moments, baffled; but then he meets an elderly traveller (a pedant) and persuades him to pretend to be Vincentio (Lucentio's father) so that the marriage can be arranged.

Petruchio, having married Katarina, sets out to make her meek and obedient. After a terrible journey, they arrive at Petruchio's house. Food is brought, but Petruchio finds fault with it, and poor Katarina has to go hungry. He then finds fault with the way the bed has been made, with the result that his wife is obliged to sit up all night in the cold. He orders new clothes for her, but when they are delivered he declares that they are badly made and ill fitting, and refuses to let her wear them. At last, weak from hunger and lack of sleep, she consents to return with him to Baptista's house. It is at this point that she finally gives in to him: Petruchio looks up at the sun, and calls it the moon; Kate, realising that further argument is useless, says:

> Forward I pray, since we have come so far,
> And be it moon, or sun, or what you please;
> And if you please to call it a rush candle,
> Henceforth I vow it shall be so for me.

It is now that the two stories meet and link up. Tranio has presented the imposter as Vincentio, and Lucentio and Bianca have crept away secretly to be married; but now Petruchio and Kate meet the real Vincentio, and take him along with them to Baptista's house. When the two Vincentios meet, there is an amusing quarrel, made more amusing by the fact that everyone is inclined to believe the imposter, and drag the real Vincentio off to prison. But all is well; Bianca and Lucentio, returning from church, interrupt the quarrel, and Baptista, seeing that the real Lucentio is a gentleman, and the real Vincentio is wealthy, is ready at once to accept the situation. Tranio becomes a servant again, and preparations are made to celebrate the wedding.

The action, as far as the two couples are concerned, is now over. But Shakespeare has one more scene for us. It is a feast, at which *three* couples are celebrating: Petruchio and Katarina, Lucentio and Bianca, Hortensio and his widow (a surly creature with a sharp tongue). When the women are out of the room, the men lay bets as to who has the most obedient wife; and, naturally, everyone present thinks Petruchio has got the worst of the bargain. He challenges the others, who both send for their wives —in vain, for the women refuse to come. But Katarina comes meekly and obediently, brings the other "froward" wives along with her, and then reads them a little lesson in how to be a good wife:

> Thy husband is thy lord, thy life, thy keeper,
> Thy head, thy sovereign; one that cares for thee,
> And for thy maintenance. Commits his body
> To painful labour, both by sea and land:
> To watch the night in storms, the day in cold,
> While thou liest warm at home, secure and safe,
> And craves no other tribute at thy hands,
> But love, fair looks, and true obedience . . .

The "Two Houses" of comedy

This kind of comedy dates back to over 200 years before the birth of Christ. In the Greek open-air theatres, on large platform stages built for the performance of the great tragedies, gay comedy was being played. But, instead of the impressive pillars with their huge centre door, through which Oedipus and Agamemnon made their entrances, Greek comedy used two smaller doors, one at either side, which came to represent two public buildings, or two houses in the same town or city.

If you look at a picture of an Elizabethan theatre you will see at once the similarity to the Greek. The English theatre was tiny in comparison to the vast amphitheatres used by the Greeks; but the open platform, with its entrances at each side of a small "inner" stage, its raised balcony, and its main acting area jutting out into the audience, offered very much the same scope for free movement as the Greek theatre.

Playwrights (and audiences) in Shakespeare's time were not as fussy about scene changes as we are today. For most of the play, one of the two doors would represent the house of Baptista, the other the house of Hortensio; the "apron" stage would then serve as the interior or exterior of either house, or for the street in between. Every scene in a Shakespeare play ends with all the actors leaving the stage, so it would be a simple matter—once the audience had got the idea—to indicate, by using different entrances, where the next scene was to take place. You will notice that every scene up to the end of the third act takes place in Padua, close to Baptista's house, and so this arrangement would work very well indeed.

However, Act IV brings a change. We are now in Petruchio's

house, waiting for Petruchio to return with his bride. Remembering that the scene before this was the one in which Petruchio carried Katarina off, we are not surprised, when we find Grumio shouting for the servants to prepare the house, light the fires and "fall in for inspection", to find that we are in Petruchio's house. To make this even more obvious, Shakespeare introduces us to a number of characters (Curtis, Nathaniel, and so on) whom we have never seen before, and none of whom appear in any of the scenes in Padua.

There are three scenes only in Petruchio's house, after which the play moves back to Padua. We are once more outside Baptista's house, and now the "upper stage" is used, as Vincentio knocks at the door and the false Vincentio appears at the window. The rest of the play takes place in Baptista's house; in fact, it is the final wedding feast, at which all the main characters are present. The whole stage is needed for this, and now the "two doors" serve another purpose: one leads to the adjacent room to which the ladies withdraw after dinner, and the other leads to the bedroom, to which Petruchio and Katarina retire at the end of the play.

Presenting the play today

A modern producer of *The Taming of the Shrew* could do worse than follow the example given above. The two houses can be placed at the sides of the stage, giving plenty of room in between for quick and lively movement; gay, Italian houses, with brightly-painted shutters, a bench or a garden seat in front of one or both of them, and a bright sky lit at the back. On this basic set, without breaks between scenes, the whole of the first three acts can be played.

They take about an hour; and, since the third act ends with a wedding, and the scene has to move away from Padua for the first time, this seems an obvious place to have the interval. During this, the bright sky can be shut off by a curtain, the shutters closed, and a table brought on; and, when the curtain rises again, the audience will readily believe that we have now moved to Petruchio's house. This is where we meet Petruchio's bunch of fumbling, incompetent servants, who (if their master is to be believed) are not worth their keep. But if they will not work for

Petruchio, they can be very useful to the producer, for they can help him to re-set the scene in Padua for the remainder of the play.

When it comes to the final scene, we have a distinct advantage over the Elizabethans. They performed in the open air, and their only illumination was the sun; we can vary the lighting of our stages, for even the poorest of acting platforms will have some lighting equipment. So far, apart from the scenes in the house of Petruchio, every scene has been bright and sunny, to suit the climate of southern Italy and the mood of the play; now the feast in Baptista's house can be made gay with lanterns and warm evening light. Indeed, if the producer wishes, the scene can be played out of doors, and now the romantic effect of moonlight can be added to the bright glow of lanterns and torches. The scenery, of course, remains the same, as it has throughout the whole play, except for very minor modifications.

You will have noticed that, at one point, I have suggested that the actors themselves should help to change the scene. This kind of trick is reasonable in Shakespeare, especially since each scene begins and ends with an empty stage. For example, it seems quite natural, in *Macbeth*, for a servant to bring on a chair for Macbeth to sit on, and to remove it at the end of the scene; or, in *The Merchant of Venice*, for the three caskets to be held by three page-boys, who would simply carry them off when they are no longer needed.

There are obviously many different ways of putting Shakespeare on the stage, and not all of them are as simple as this. A great deal of spectacular effect can be achieved by the use of revolving platforms, gauzes, hydraulic lifts, and elaborate lighting consoles, but the important thing to remember is that, if you do not have all these expensive refinements, it does not really matter. Plays by Shakespeare do not need them; on the other hand, even the simplest of settings has to be well designed and carefully constructed.

Bringing the play to life

There is a lot of pleasure to be had from acting Shakespeare. Many thousands of people who would never dream of reading a play (especially a Shakespeare play) go every year to see his plays acted. Actors love Shakespeare, because he gives them larger-than-life characters to play, and splendid lines to speak. The producer finds the plays full of action, and humour, and exciting movement. To many people—and particularly to those who are obliged to study them for examinations—the words appear dead on the printed page, but suddenly come to life in a performance.

The first difficulty for most people, when it comes to acting the plays, is the *language*. Many of the words and expressions are unfamiliar; and, to make matters worse, the majority of the speeches are in verse. The text has little or nothing in the way of stage directions—merely the speeches, and the divisions into acts and scenes, and even these divisions were not put there by Shakespeare, but were added by editors at a time when it was fashionable for plays—especially tragedies—to have five acts. Now, this last point gives us a clue about how to deal with the problems of acting Shakespeare. If the acts and scenes were not put there by the author, let us forget about them, playing the scenes without a break, and having the intervals when it suits us. This is precisely what happens at Stratford, or in any other professional production of the plays, for there are sometimes scenes so short that to separate them from the rest of the play would be silly.

Next, what about the verse? The difficulty here is a purely imaginary one. There is, after all, no reason why a speech should be any less actable because it is written out in an unusual way. Shakespeare—and many other playwrights—used verse because they believed it made the speech sound more impressive and dignified, but it was never their intention to make it more difficult to understand. Here are some examples; judge for yourself.

First, Lucentio, arranging with Tranio to change places: say the speech quickly, eagerly, like a conspirator, and you will see that it goes in a series of short bursts, each one a new point, and that the poetry—if we can call it so—does not really affect the meaning at all, but actually *helps* us to speak the lines:

> . . . We have not yet been seen in any house,
> Nor can we be distinguish'd by our faces,
> For man or master; then it follows thus:

> Thou shalt be master, Tranio, in my stead;
> Keep house, and port, and servants, as I should;
> I will some other be, some Florentine,
> Some Neapolitan, or meaner man of Pisa.
> 'Tis hatch'd, and shall be so: Tranio, at once
> Uncase thee; take my coloured hat and cloak.
> When Biondello comes, he waits on thee,
> But I will charm him first to keep his tongue.

Does it matter that the word "port" is unusual here? or that "charm" is not given its more familiar meaning? The *intention* of the speech is quite obvious—and you must remember that the people who go to see Shakespeare on the stage do not take their dictionaries with them.

Here now is Katarina, the shrew. She is furious that Petruchio has not turned up on the wedding day, and she has quite decided that he is staying away deliberately in order to make a fool of her. She is in a fine old rage; and, as long as the speech is said angrily (and a little tearfully as well) the meaning is quite clear:

> No shame but mine, I must forsooth be forc'd
> To give my hand oppos'd against my heart
> Unto a mad-brain rudesby, full of spleen,
> Who woo'd in haste, and means to wed at leisure:
> I told you, I, he was a frantic fool,
> Hiding his bitter jests in blunt behaviour,
> And to be noted for a merry man;
> He'll woo a thousand, 'point the day of marriage,
> Make friends, invite, and proclaim the banns,
> Yet never means to wed where he hath woo'd:
> Now must the world point at poor Katherine,
> And say, lo, there is mad Petruchio's wife,
> If it would please him come and marry her.

It is not difficult to sound angry when there are lines like these to help.

Lastly, we come to this problem of *stage directions*. Entrances and exits are usually indicated in the text, but all other kinds of "stage business' have to be guessed at. Of course, it is part of the producer's job, whatever the play, to put in additional actions which he thinks will help the performance, add to the humour, or increase the dramatic effect; these bits of "business" will vary from one production to another, and would not be in the text in any case. All the other actions—what we might call the "essential business"—can be worked out quite easily, simply by reading the scene. Here, in Act IV, Scene 1, Petruchio has entered with his new bride. He has shouted and bullied the servants, finding fault with everything; we can imagine what a state of panic they are all in. Then we get this:

PETRUCHIO: Go rascals go, and fetch my supper in.
(Servants go out)
Where is the life that late I led?
Where are those—Sit down, Kate,
And welcome. Soud, soud, soud, soud . . .
(Enter servants with supper)
Why, when I say? Nay good sweet Kate, be merry.
Pull off my boots, you rogues; you villains, when!
It was a friar of orders grey,
As he forth walked on his way.
Out you rogue, you pluck my foot awry,
Take that, and mend the plucking off the other.
Be merry, Kate; some water here: what hoa!
(Enter one with water)
Where's my spaniel Troilus? Sirrah, get you hence,
And bid my cousin Ferdinand come hither:
One, Kate, that you must kiss and be acquainted with.
Where are my slippers? Shall I have some water?
Come Kate and wash, and welcome heartily.
You whoreson villain, will you let it fall?

KATARINA: Patience I pray you, 'twas a fault unwilling.

PETRUCHIO: A whorcson beetle-headed flap-eared knave:
Come Kate, sit down, I know you have a stomach;
Will you give thanks, sweet Kate, or else shall I?
What's this: mutton?

1st SERVANT: Aye.

PETRUCHIO: Who brought it?

2nd SERVANT: I.

PETRUCHIO: 'Tis burnt, and so is all the meat:
What dogs are these, where is the rascal cook?
How durst you villains bring it from the dresser
And serve it thus to me who love it not?
There, take it to you, trenchers, cups and all:
You heedless joltheads and unmanner'd slaves.
What, do you grumble? I'll be with you straight.

On the line: "Where is the life . . ." and, later, "There was a friar . . ." we guess that Petruchio is singing to himself. This helps us to picture him lolling in a chair, shouting impatiently at the poor servants. To show how unreasonable he is, we see him shouting for supper, and for water, *after* the servants have brought them in. We can tell that, on the words: "Take that . . ." he strikes the unfortunate fellow who is trying to pull off his boots; and it is a reasonable guess that he deliberately knocks the water-jug out of the servant's hands, and then curses him for being clumsy. In the last speech quoted, he first jumps up in a rage; then he throws the food (and the crockery) at the terrified servants; he chases them out of the room; then, hearing a murmur of protest from one or two of them, he turns back with a further threat.

Precisely how Petruchio moves about the stage, and what comic trips and stumbles the servants perform, is a matter for the individual actor or producer; but there is sufficient clue in the lines, without any stage directions whatever, for us to imagine the scene. And, if we can imagine it, we can perform it.

Comic characters and comic business

Most of the characters in this play are straightforward. Baptista is a bit of a miser, and Gremio, the old man, is a stock figure of fun; but most of the young men in the play are well-to-do, polished, and likeable. In contrast to these elegant young noblemen, there are a bunch of low comedy characters—a tailor and a haberdasher, a couple of clowns (Grumio and Biondello), and a houseful of comic servants (Curtis, Nathaniel, and the rest). Odd voices, odd clothes, odd ways of walking or standing, these are all possible ways of making these types more amusing, and it would certainly be a dull play if these comic characters were played "straight". Sometimes, too, the producer introduces a piece of "comic business" to squeeze more laughs out of the situation.

Funny tricks of this kind are worthwhile, (a) if they are really funny, without detracting from the scene; (b) if they are "in character"—that is, if they are the sort of thing such a character would do. Here is an example, from a production of this play, of an effective piece of "comic business":

Petruchio is waiting to meet Katarina for the first time. When she enters, he is sitting on a stool; and, determined to be impolite, he remains seated. Furiously, she comes up to him and kicks the stool from under him; but Petruchio is ready for her, and remains balanced, with an insolent smile on his face. Round One, you might say, to Petruchio. It gets its laugh, of course; but it also helps to launch the "battle" which is to follow.

A Shakespeare play, whether serious or comic, can very easily sound like a dull recital of set speeches unless some effort is made to give feeling, and movement, to the performance. We must never forget that, whether they speak in verse or prose, the characters are meant to represent living people, with real emotions, and that when they are angry, or pleased, or frightened, their behaviour should be recognisable. The little scene which follows is not remotely funny unless the actress playing Katarina remembers that, since she married Petruchio, she has not slept, not eaten, not been allowed to change her clothes, and is so weary of being ill-treated that she has—for the moment—lost all her old pride and independence. Grumio, on the other hand, is quite deliberately tormenting her. She is begging him for something to eat.

GRUMIO: No, no forsooth I dare not for my life.
KATARINA: The more my wrong, the more his spite appears.
What, did he marry me to famish me?
Beggars that come unto my father's door,
Upon entreaty have a present alms,
If not, elsewhere they meet with charity:
But I, who never knew how to entreat,
Nor never needed that I should entreat,
Am starv'd for meat, giddy with lack of sleep,
With oaths kept waking, and with brawling fed,
And that which spites me more than all these wants,
He does it under name of perfect love;
As who should say, if I should sleep or eat
'Twere deadly sickness, or else present death.
I prithee go, and get me some repast,
I care not what, so it be wholesome food.
GRUMIO: What say you to a neat's foot?
KATARINA: 'Tis passing good, I prithee let me have it.
GRUMIO: I fear it is too choleric a meat.
How say you to a fat tripe finely broil'd?
KATARINA: I like it well, good Grumio fetch it me.
GRUMIO: I cannot tell, I fear 'tis choleric.
What say you to a piece of beef and mustard?
KATARINA: A dish that I do love to feed upon.
GRUMIO: Ay, but the mustard is too hot a little.

KATARINA: Why then the beef, and let the mustard rest.
GRUMIO: Nay then I will not, you shall have the mustard
Or else you get no beef of Grumio.
KATARINA: Then both or one, or anything thou wilt.
GRUMIO: Why then, the mustard without the beef.
KATARINA: Go get thee gone, thou false deluding slave
That feed'st me with the very name of meat.
Sorrow on thee, and all the pack of you
That triumph thus upon my misery . . .

Proud Kate—the bullying, scolding girl of the first three acts, is now so desperate that she is even begging favours from the servants. Can you see her, turning on all her charm to persuade Grumio to give her something to eat? And can you hear him, lingering over the "fat tripe" and the "beef and mustard" until her mouth is watering. He probably pauses before each delicacy, in order to lead her on a little further; then, with a sudden ". . . the mustard without the beef" he skips off with a mischievous laugh. Kate loses her temper completely—her patience was exhausted long since—and she rushes after him, cursing the whole "pack" of servants, and furious enough to pull out Grumio's hair by the roots—if she could catch him.

A lot of the pleasure in acting Shakespeare comes from realising what the characters are thinking and feeling, and then working out the ways of representing these thoughts and emotions in performance.

Two scenes of lively action

When Petruchio comes to marry Katarina, his violent courtship reaches a climax. The whole of this very amusing scene (Act III, Scene 2) is worth looking at.

A: THE WEDDING

We have first of all a worried Baptista and an angry Kate, for it looks as if Petruchio is not coming. Then comes Biondello, who, in a long rigmarole full of stable-boy's slang, describes how Petruchio is approaching, dressed in rags, and riding a decrepit old horse. Petruchio enters, sweeps all objections aside, and rushes off to the church, followed by most of the company.

For a few moments, Tranio and Lucentio remain alone, and exchange a few words about Lucentio's hopes of marrying

Bianca. Old Gremio then appears, and describes the disgraceful behaviour of Petruchio in the church; then back come all the other characters, and stand amazed as Petruchio invites them all to his wedding feast, and then, despite his bride's protests, carries her off, leaving the rest of the party to make what they can of the affair.

B: PETRUCHIO'S HOUSE

This scene (Act IV, Scene 1) follows the previous one. Grumio arrives, sent on ahead to warn the servants of Petruchio's approach. He describes for us the hazards of the journey, and we are ready for the sore, weary and travel-stained Kate, and the bullying, swearing Petruchio. The scene includes the serving of the supper (part of which is quoted earlier), and ends with Kate being carried off, unwashed and supperless, to bed.

This is a splendid scene to practise the use of a comic crowd. Most of the servants have little or nothing to say, but their behaviour is an essential part of the humour of the scene.

2. The Playboy of the Western World

by JOHN MILLINGTON SYNGE

(*J. M. Synge was born in 1871, in a little village close to Dublin, in Ireland. Although he lived some of his short life in Paris, he was by temperament a countryman, and he was happiest when travelling by bicycle through the remote country districts, staying with the farmers and fisherfolk, and talking with tramps and tinkers. He also spent some time on the island of Aran, a wild and rocky place where, many years before, his uncle had been a Protestant curate.*

All the characters in Synge's plays are very simple people, getting a hard living from farming or fishing. In most cases, the people he met on his wanderings lived very cramped lives, never moving more than a mile or two from one spot, and knowing nothing of the way of life in other parts of the country. They were used to hardship, for their livelihood often depended upon the luck of the weather; and, although they were mostly devoutly Catholic, their lives were steeped in folklore and superstition. In this play, Synge imagines what might happen when a small rural community, placidly following its petty routine existence, is suddenly stirred up by the arrival of a stranger who brings a little excitement into their lives.

For a short time (he died in 1909, aged only 38) Synge was one of a small group of writers who were trying to re-awaken an interest in the Irish theatre. They founded a "national theatre" for Irish plays—the Abbey Theatre, in Dublin—but when The Playboy of the Western World *was first performed there in 1907 there were riots at the performance. Many people in the audience, and many critics afterwards, thought the play an insult to the fair name of Ireland. Certainly, it makes fun of the simplicity of the people, their narrow outlook, and their naïve attitude to religion; but it is hard to see, when the laughter has died away, what all the fuss was about.*)

The setting of the story

There is nothing difficult about the play, but it helps a little if we know something about the setting. The action takes place in a "shebeen"—described by the author as "a country public-house"—but it is very different from a public house in England. It is as much a farmhouse as an ale-house, for a good deal of the livelihood of the owner comes from grazing a few sheep and goats, and cultivating a little plot of land. For the rest, the shebeen is partly a public house, partly a shop, and in this village—as in many others—it is the meeting-place of all the men from several miles around.

Very important in this play is the part played by religion in the lives of the characters. Synge, though a Protestant, understood and respected the trust placed by these country folk in the parish priest, and the constant fear they had of doing anything to offend the Mother Church. In one speech, close to the beginning of the play, Pegeen (the heroine) has this to say:

> It's a wonder, Shaneen, the Holy Father'd be taking notice of the likes of you; for if I was him I wouldn't bother with this place where you'll meet none but Red Linahan has a squint in his eye, and Patcheen is lame in his heel, or the mad Mulrannies were driven from California and they lost in their wits. We're a queer lot these times to go troubling the Holy Father on his sacred seat.

Shaneen (Shawn Keogh) has applied for a "dispensation" to marry Pegeen, and he is waiting anxiously for the church's permission so that the wedding can take place. This speech, like so many more in the play, shows us how unimportant this village is, and how rarely anything exciting or unusual happens. The people are even a little bored with being good: as one of the girls says:

> . . . There's a pair do fit me well, and I'll be keeping them for walking to the priest, when you'd be ashamed this place, going up winter and summer with nothing worth while to confess at all.

A large part of the joke is that this god-fearing people make a hero out of a self-confessed murderer.

One of the things which probably offended the original audience was the amount of drunkenness the play contains. The Irish have a widespread reputation for being fond of the bottle, and this play does nothing to discourage the idea. However, they have an excuse; for, at the beginning of the play, the menfolk are off to "Kate Cassidy's wake"—and, as everyone knows, a wake is a grand excuse to consume a quantity of drink, especially as the drink is provided free of charge by the sorrowing relatives of the deceased. By an odd coincidence, the wake is followed by the village sports—another festive occasion, on which a man could hardly be blamed for drinking a little more than usual.

The story of the play

ACT I: It is evening, and Pegeen Mike (Margaret Flaherty, daughter of the landlord, Michael James) is ordering goods for her wedding to Shawn Keogh. The men of the village, including Michael James himself, are preparing to go to a wake, and Pegeen is grumbling at being left in the house all night by herself. Michael James suggests that Shawn should stay; but poor Shawn, terrified lest the priest should have something to say about his spending the night alone in the same house as Pegeen, is determined to go home to bed. He rushes off, in spite of Michael James's attempts to stop him, but he is back within seconds with the news that a strange young man is approaching the house. This is Christy Mahon, worn out from travelling, and lack of food; a mysterious character, at first unwilling to say who he is, where he is from, or what he has done to be afraid of the police—as he obviously is. The others gather round him, guessing at first one crime, then another; at last, goaded by Pegeen, he confesses that he has murdered his father.

PEGEEN: You did nothing at all. A soft lad the like of you wouldn't slit the windpipe of a screeching sow.
CHRISTY: You're not speaking the truth.
PEGEEN: Not speaking the truth, is it? Would you have me knock the head of you with the butt of the broom?
CHRISTY: Don't strike me. I killed my father, Tuesday was a week, for doing the like of that.

However, as he seems such a decent fellow, and his father (doubt-less) asked for it, the company is more delighted than shocked at the news. He is, moreover, the ideal man to stay and protect Pegeen from criminals while the menfolk go off to the wake, and he is promptly made potboy, and offered a bed by the fire. Shawn, seeing that there is now another man in the house, offers to stay to look after Pegeen, but she sends him packing. Pegeen is quite fascinated by this stranger, but their cosy chat is interrupted by the arrival of Widow Quin, with the story that Shawn and Father Reilly have suggested that she should take Christy to stay at her house; for, she says " 'It isn't fitting' says the priesteen, 'to have his likeness lodging with an orphaned girl'."

But Pegeen, having got the stranger to herself, is reluctant to let him go so easily. The Widow turns on her charm; Pegeen starts to abuse the Widow. Christy, given the choice, prefers to stay where he is, and Widow Quin retreats—for the moment. Christy, seeing the warm fire, and the blankets, and the pretty girl, cannot believe his luck:

> Well, it's a clean bed and soft with it, and it's great luck and company I've won me in the end of time—two fine women fighting for the likes of me—till I'm thinking this night wasn't I a foolish fellow not to kill my father in the years gone by.

ACT II: The following morning. Christy is having a wash, but hides away when four young girls come in. They have heard stories of the man who killed his father, and they have come to see for themselves. They meet Christy, and press gifts upon him, and are giggling happily at their new hero when Widow Quin enters. Together they persuade him to tell again the story of his great exploit, which he does very readily, delighted to have found such a good audience. The girls see him as a fit man to be the next husband for Widow Quin, but this idyll is cut short by Pegeen's entrance. She sends her rivals packing once more; and once more (as she did the night before) encourages Christy to pay her compliments, and to think about staying on in the house. Back comes the Widow Quin, with Shawn Keogh; and having got Pegeen out of the house for a few moments to tend her straying sheep, Shawn tries to bribe Christy to leave the district. Christy takes the bribe (a suit of new clothes) but shows no signs of intending to leave; so the Widow Quin offers to try to make Christy marry her, leaving the way clear for Shawn and Pegeen to be married. She is making little headway, for Christy is now so full of his own importance that there is no hope of influencing him:

> From this out I'll have no want of company when all sorts is bringing me
> their food and clothing, the way they'd set their eyes upon a gallant
> orphan cleft his father with one blow to the breeches belt . . .

But Christy's triumph is brief, for in at the door comes Mahon,
Christy's father, his head swathed in bandages. He doesn't see
Christy, but he has a revealing talk with Widow Quin, who
discovers what a poor soul the wandering hero really is:

> . . . and wasn't he the laughing joke of every female woman where four
> baronies meet, the way the girls would stop their weeding if they seen him
> coming the road to let a roar at him and call him the looney of Mahon's.

The Widow Quin sends Mahon off on a false scent, much to the
relief of the terrified Christy; and starts once again to try to
wheedle him into marrying her. But Christy is set on Pegeen,
and—as the girls come up the hill to take him down to the sports
—the widow agrees to keep silent about his father, provided, of
course, she gets something for herself out of the affair.

ACT III: Old Mahon, Christy's father, has not gone very far.
Two of the men from the wake, Philly and Jimmy, are sitting in
the shebeen when the old man comes in, and tells them that his
son tried to split his skull. In comes the Widow Quin, and
manages to convince the two men that Mahon is raving; but
now we hear the cheers from the green below, and all four of
them crowd to the window to watch the races. Christy wins, and
is carried shoulder-high by the excited villagers up towards the
house. This time Mahon swears he recognises his son, but once
again the widow convinces him that he is suffering from delusions,
and manages to get him out of the way before Christy arrives.

Once Pegeen gets Christy to herself, the two of them agree to
be married. Shawn is given his marching orders, and Pegeen's
father, Michael James, is asked to pronounce his blessing upon
Christy and Pegeen. This is how he ends his stirring speech:

> . . . A daring fellow is the jewel of the world, and a man did split his
> father's middle with a single clout should have the bravery of ten, so may
> God and Mary and St. Patrick bless you, and increase you from this
> mortal day.

At this vital moment, old Mahon rushes in. Now the secret is out,
and Pegeen is full of contempt for her hero. Mahon orders

THE PLAYBOY OF THE WESTERN WORLD

Christy to come with him, but the boy snatches up a turf-spade from the door, and chases the old man outside. There is a blow; a yell; then silence. It looks as though Christy has really done this time what he only boasted of doing before.

Foolishly, Christy expects everyone—especially Pegeen—to be pleased. After all, didn't they all love him when they *thought* he had killed his father? Well, now he has done it. But the Widow Quin knows better, and tries to get him to run away before it is too late. Back come the crowd, this time with a rope, and they are all set to tie him up and carry him off to justice. Shawn (brave enough when he has friends at his back) is there too, and there follows a crazy tug-of-war, with Christy and the menfolk at opposite ends of the rope. Their struggles are interrupted by the entrance—yet again—of old Mahon. He is still not dead, but he is more than a little bewildered at the way his foolish son has turned on him. For Christy, this is the "moment of truth"—he realises that he can master the old man; he realises, too, that all the honour and glory he had with Pegeen and the others is finished for ever. So he decides to cut his losses, and leave for home:

> Ten thousand blessings on all that's here, for you've turned me a likely gaffer in the end of all, the way I'll go romancing through a romping lifetime from this hour to the dawning of the judgment day.

So saying, off he goes. Shawn, relieved that his rival has quit the field, quite naturally assumes that he has no further problems:

SHAWN: It's a miracle Father Reilly can wed us in the end of all, and we'll have none to trouble us when his vicious bite is healed.

PEGEEN: (*hitting him a box on the ear*) Quit my sight. (*Putting her shawl over her head and breaking into wild lamentations*) Oh, my grief, I've lost him surely. I've lost the only Playboy of the Western World.

The shape of the play

· This play is written to a pattern which you will find in many other plays, although their actual plots, their characters, and their intentions may be quite different. Into the play, during the first act, comes a stranger—a character from a different way of life—whose coming affects the lives of several of the main characters; he stays for a short while, and a number of things happen simply because he is there; then, in the last act, he goes on his way, but things are not quite as they would have been if he had not been there.

Before Christy makes his appearance, the author introduces us to the main characters in his story. It is important that we see what a weakling Shawn Keogh is, and how bored with her small existence Pegeen has become, so that we are ready, when the "playboy" arrives, for him to be welcomed as a better alternative. We see and hear the simple wonderment of the peasants in the shebeen when Christy is telling his story, and so we are not surprised when they, and the young village girls in the second act, look up to Christy as a kind of dashing hero. To the Widow Quin, alone in her little house since her husband died, he comes like the answer to a prayer.

Old Mahon's arrival, in the second act, does two very important things: it lets us know what sort of a man Christy really is, and it prepares us for the fact that the hero-worship cannot go on for very long. A good play will always contain some indication of the way events are likely to go, so that, as we watch it working its way towards its conclusion, we can feel that this *had* to happen. With Mahon alive, Christy is not a hero-murderer, but a clumsy, boasting liar; with Mahon "killed" in front of the horrified eyes of the villagers, Christy is no longer a hero—just a murderer, a criminal who must be brought to justice.

The interesting thing about the two main characters, Pegeen and Christy, is that they are surprisingly alike. Certainly Pegeen is a strong, independent girl, and Christy a rather weak, effeminate character; but they are both full of romantic ideas, and ready to picture themselves doing great and glorious things. Christy beat his father over the head because he was sick and tired of the same dull existence, and Pegeen turns from the stick-in-the-mud Shawn to the "playboy" for the same reason.

Christy and Pegeen are not the only ones to exaggerate, to romance, to build castles in the air. Everybody does it, and you have a feeling throughout the play that, in order to make life more exciting, more amusing, and more wonderful, each character sees no harm in embroidering the truth a little to make it sound more important. With bated breath, they tell each other stories of strange doings which have been handed on from one teller to another, gaining a little more fantasy with each telling. Because they are simple country people, they take everything very seriously. Listen to Shawn, protesting vigorously at Michael James:

> Leave me go, Michael James, leave me go you old Pagan, leave me go, or I'll get the curse of the priests on you, and of the scarlet-coated bishops of the Courts of Rome.

And here is Jimmy Farrell, telling the tale to Philly:

> JIMMY: . . . Did you never hear tell of the skulls they have in the city of Dublin, ranged out like blue jugs in a cabin of Connaught?
> PHILLY: And you believe that?
> JIMMY: Didn't a lad see them and he after coming from harvesting in the Liverpool boat? "They have them there," says he, "making a show of the great people there was one time walking the world. White skulls and black skulls and yellow skulls, and some with full teeth, and some haven't only but one."

When old Mahon is convinced by Widow Quin that he is out of his mind, he is not a bit put out—in fact, he is rather proud of it:

> Then I'd best be going to the union beyond, and there'll be a welcome before me I tell you, and I a terrible and fearful case, the way that there I was one time, screeching in a straightened waistcoat, with seven doctors writing out my sayings in a printed book. Would you believe that?

You will find many examples of this kind of talk. What makes the play so comic, apart from the absurd situations, is this talent that all its characters have for thinking themselves important.

The speech of the characters

> When I was writing *The Shadow of the Glen* some years ago, I got more aid than any learning could have given me from a chink in the floor of the old Wicklow house where I was staying, that let me hear what was being said by the servant girls in the kitchen.

These words appear in Synge's preface to *The Playboy of the Western World*, and they explain very well how he came to write this quaint, sing-song English which all his characters speak. It is not poetry; but it most certainly is not prose as most of us know it. Very often in plays the characters say the kind of clever things that we would all like to say, but we never seem to be able to think of them; Synge's characters speak a lilting, poetic English which is based on the dialects of Ireland—though no Wicklow servant girl ever talked quite so grandly as some of Synge's characters do.

Once we are used to the style of speaking, there is nothing at all difficult about Synge's language. If we want to perform the plays, it is quite unnecessary to put on a "stage Irish" voice, since the rhythms of the speeches, and the words themselves, give the play all the country flavour it needs. For not only have the speeches a singing rhythm of their own, but the words themselves are full of talk of the weather, and the countryside, and a farmer's life.

Oddly enough, there are very few Irish words in the play, and the few that there are prevent no real problem. A "loy"—the weapon with which Christy struck his father—is a turf-spade, rather like a garden spade, but with a longer blade for digging down into the soft peat; "poteen" is a local whisky, made from potatoes, and distilled in odd corners of Ireland—quite illegally —as a stronger alternative to "porter"—that is, Irish beer. But words like these are quite rare, and there is no misunderstanding the play on their account.

There are, however, a considerable number of words to which the Irish suffix "-een" has been added. This is another way of saying "little" or "dear" (other languages do this sort of thing: "chanson*ette*"—a little song; "Kav*ichko*"—a little cup of coffee; "lieb*chen*"—little darling; and so on). We have the word already in "shebeen"—a little house; and the play has a number more, like "supeen"—a little drink; "cnuceen"—a little hill; "Shaneen" —little Shawn. You can see now how the heroine, Margaret Flaherty, comes to be called "Pegeen Mike". She is Pegeen (little, or young, Peggy) from her first name, Margaret; and Mike because her father is called Michael.

The effect of this style of writing is to make even the most harrowing speeches sound musical, and to leave us with the impression that all the characters love to hear the sound of their own voices. This is only human: Christy enjoys telling the girls how he came to kill his father, and Mahon enjoys telling the Widow Quin what a hard time he has had of it. Philly Cullen and Jimmy Farrell enjoy the gruesome tales they tell to each other, and the audience thoroughly enjoys listening to them.

Two scenes from the play

(1) ACT I, from the entrance of Christy ("God save all here") to the departure of the men for Kate Cassidy's wake. A pleasant scene, with a small crowd of men drinking and talking: then the entry of the stranger, and the gradual build-up of interest as we hear a little about him; then the chorus of excitement as it is discovered that he is, in fact, a murderer.

(2) ACT II, from the beginning of the scene. Now it is the girls' turn. Christy is up and about; and, though it is early in the morning, the curiosity of the village maidens has brought them to the shebeen before breakfast. Their childish excitement, Christy's shyness and his gradual increase in confidence, the "betrothal" to Widow Quin—sharply interrupted by Pegeen's furious entrance—all make a very good scene.

TERM SIX

A famous masterpiece

Hamlet by WILLIAM SHAKESPEARE

Hamlet

by WILLIAM SHAKESPEARE

(Of the thirty-seven plays usually attributed to Shakespeare, four are commonly grouped together under the title of "mature tragedies". They are Hamlet, Othello, King Lear, *and* Macbeth, *and each tells the story of the downfall and death of the central character. Each of these "tragic heroes" is basically a noble and a good man, who meets his unfortunate end partly through his own mistakes, partly as a result of the unlucky circumstances in which he finds himself.*

All four plays are popular, are frequently performed, and even more frequently written about, but none of them has attracted as much attention as Hamlet. *The hero of the play, Hamlet himself, is a complicated person, a mixture of moods—even contradictions—and because of this the part is a great challenge to professional actors. For much the same reason, and also because the play as a whole seems to probe deeply into the problems of human nature, hundreds of books, articles and essays have been written about the play.*

Unperturbed by the cry that Hamlet *is "difficult", "obscure", or even "unactable", thousands of people have seen the play in the theatre and have enjoyed it enormously. While it would be unreasonable to ignore the many wise things which have been said about the play, it remains true that, for most people, what matters is how exciting it is to watch. On this score the play is a tremendous success.)*

Most good editions of the separate plays of Shakespeare have excellent notes clearing up some of the difficulties of meaning, explaining references which seem strange to modern readers, and generally helping those wishing to read or act the play to find their way about it. I am suggesting that you might enjoy reading most of the play, and acting quite large parts of it; and that, in order to do this, you will possess yourselves of a properly edited text. What follows, then, is not a set of explanatory notes, such as the editions already have, but a few introductory facts which you might find useful. The rest of this chapter is a kind of "conducted tour" through the play, with particular emphasis on those matters which make the play interesting and exciting to act and to see. Of course, many of the interesting and controversial ideas which critics and scholars have at various times raised are often brought out by a particular performance or production, because actors and producers have their own "theories" about the play, and these will affect the way they do their job.

The words on the page

Nowadays, when a book is published, everything which the author writes is carefully printed, and then a copy is sent to him to make sure that no mistakes have been made. His wishes are not only respected with regard to the text, but his advice is heeded on such matters as headings, size of print, and—in certain cases—the arrangement of the words on the page. If the book happens to be a play, the publisher may print the text as the author first wrote it, or he may print a revised text, based on the author's experience of the play's first performance. However, whichever he does, the publisher will exercise just as much care as he would over any other kind of book, and there is little doubt that the finished product is the text as the writer intended it.

No such foolproof system existed in Shakespeare's time. Many of the "first editions" of Shakespeare (and this is particularly true of *Hamlet*) were *pirated*—that is, they were printed from shorthand notes, or from borrowed copies of the play-scripts, and they were produced entirely without the permission (let alone the assistance) of the author. Later editions were sometimes so different that they actually resembled different versions of the play altogether; but, just to make matters worse, even the "bad" versions contained interesting—and possibly genuine—lines and speeches that did not appear in the later texts. The first collected edition of Shakespeare's complete works (usually known as the First Folio Edition) appeared in 1623; but, even if we assume that this is the most accurate text, some of the words are so badly printed that one can only guess at what was originally intended.

This sounds an impossible situation, but it is not as bad as it seems. Careful comparison of the Folio with the "good" quarto* editions, aided by intelligent and scholarly guesswork by the editors, has produced a text for most plays with only minor disagreements. If your copy of *Hamlet* seems to differ from mine in some of the quotations, it is because of these "minor disagreements"—most of which have little or no effect on the meaning of the speech as a whole. In fact, the whole subject need never have been brought up, but for the fact that *Hamlet* has one or two special problems of its own.

The length of the play

Shakespeare's plays vary considerably in length, but *Hamlet* happens to be very much longer than any of the others. Some of the writers who have studied the play have decided that what is actually printed is parts of *two* plays—or two versions of the same play—and that this accounts for the apparent repetitions. There is one scene, in particular, where this certainly might be true, but this we shall deal with in its proper place.

Assuming that the text of *Hamlet* is one play, and one play only, it still plays for over four hours, and so producers are faced with the problem of "cutting" it. They have to decide which scenes to leave out, which long speeches to shorten, and which parts of scenes to do away with. Experience has shown that certain of the scenes, and parts of scenes, are of little interest to a modern audience; but what to do with the rest of the text is open to wide disagreement. Sir Laurence Olivier's film version of *Hamlet* did not merely shorten the play considerably, even to the extent of leaving out certain characters; it actually altered some of the words, and changed the familiar order of some of the scenes. This kind of mutilation is quite unnecessary, however convenient it may be, and the result was not, in the end, very satisfactory.

However, it was not merely the manhandling of the text which made the Olivier *Hamlet* a poor version of Shakespeare. The play *is* usually shortened for the stage, but not always, and there have been a number of productions in which the whole play—without a single line omitted—has been given. It would be a

* "Folio" means a page formed by folding a large sheet once only; "quarto" is a sheet folded once more, to give *four* smaller pages.

poor play if it contained so many unnecessary lines that many of them could be left out without harming the original at all. If we look carefully at the play, we can see that it has to be long.

It is long, in the first place, because a vital part of the action is the hero's refusal to carry out his revenge for the murder of his father. We need time for this persistent delay to become obvious, and this would be quite impossible if the events of the play happened very quickly. A second reason for the length of the play is that it is based upon a true story of a quarrel between the kingdoms of Norway and Denmark. This political matter is discussed from time to time throughout the play; but it has hardly anything to do with Hamlet, the main character, and his particular problem. A third reason why the play is long is that Hamlet, the hero, is a great talker. He has been for some years a student, and he is a witty and fluent speaker. He talks at length to his friends and companions; he also talks to himself, in a series of "soliloquies" in which his deepest personal thoughts are spoken aloud. A fourth—and final—reason for the play's length is that a great deal happens. It may be long, but it is not dull, and every scene contributes something important to the development of the story.

A story of revenge

In 1585, or thereabouts, a play appeared called *The Spanish Tragedy*. It was written by Thomas Kyd, and it was about a father who plotted revenge against the murderers of his son. The play contained several interesting features, including: a ghost scene; a "dumb show" (a representation, without words, of part of the action); a number of "mad" scenes; a "play within a play"; and a final scene with several dead bodies upon the stage.

In 1602 the play of *Hamlet* was published. It is about a son who plots revenge against his uncle, the murderer of his father. It contains, among other things: three ghost scenes; several mad scenes, involving two of the main characters; a "dumb show"; a play within a play; and a final duel scene, involving the deaths, on the stage, of four principal characters.

In spite of these remarkable resemblances, the two plays are not at all alike in the details of their stories. but there is little doubt that the appearance of such similar scenes was not an accident. In 1612 a man called John Webster wrote a play called *The Duchess of Malfi*, in which a cardinal hired an assassin to carry out revenge upon his sister for the "crime" of marrying a second time. The avenger, Bosola, appears in a suit of black, and constantly attacks with savage speech the morals and manners of his day; Hamlet, in his "customary suits of solemn black" does exactly the same. Toward the end of the play, there is a moving scene set amid the ruins of an old chapel; toward the end of *Hamlet*, there is a scene in a graveyard. Bosola, like Hamlet, puts on an act of madness, and at one point he torments the duchess by placing her in a house full of madmen. The play ends with a bloody scene in which both sides suffer as a result of the cruel and ruthless revenge plot; *Hamlet* ends in just the same way.

There are quite a number of other plays, written about this time, which follow the same general pattern. It looks, therefore, as if Shakespeare set out to write a play of revenge, using as his main character a man tired of life, angry and unco-operative, a man with a grudge. Like the hero of *The Spanish Tragedy*, Hamlet uses a play within a play to further his purpose; and, like several other writers of revenge plays, Shakespeare introduces madness—real and pretended madness—into the action. To stir up the feelings of the audience, and to build up the atmosphere of horror, there is also a graveyard—and a ghost.

Shakespeare also made Hamlet a very complicated character, and it is this more than anything else which has caused all the fuss about the play. But, by including all the ingredients of a revenge melodrama into the play, Shakespeare has guaranteed that, while the experts are arguing about what Hamlet is really like, the rest of us can have plenty of excitement as we watch the play.

Scene by scene

Instead of a summary of the whole story, followed by comments about performance, it seems better to combine the two. Here, then, is the story of each separate scene of the play, together with a few remarks which might help you to picture the scene on the stage, or to act it—or part of it—for yourselves.

The play is set in Elsinore, the royal castle of the Kings of

Denmark. You will realise from the plot that, at the time of the play, Denmark ruled over quite a large territory, including England. This places the action before the Norman Conquest, in a much more primitive and barbarous society; but it would be as well to ignore this, because obviously Shakespeare imagined his characters as quite modern in behaviour and civilisation.

ACT I, SCENE 1: *It is night, on the battlements of Elsinore. The guard is being relieved, and with the relief comes Horatio, a student and friend of Hamlet. The soldiers have seen something these last three nights, and they have brought Horatio, who thinks they have imagined it, to see for himself. As the men describe the apparition, it comes. Horatio tries to speak to it, but it walks off. All are impressed with the fact that it greatly resembles the former king, Hamlet's father, and they wonder—being superstitious—whether it is a warning of some approaching disaster. Horatio tells them that the country is disturbed by preparations for the defence of Denmark; for, it seems, the son of the late King of Norway is trying to raise an army for the recovery of certain lands taken from his father by Hamlet's father. Now the Ghost appears again, and Horatio is about to speak with it when the cock crows, and it walks off. They then agree to tell Hamlet what they have seen, in the hope that it will speak to him.*

The first few lines set the scene perfectly:

> BERNARDO: Who's there?
> FRANCISCO: Nay, answer me; stand and unfold yourself,
> BERNARDO: Long live the King!
> FRANCISCO: Bernardo?
> BERNARDO: He.
> FRANCISCO: You come most carefully upon your hour.

Francisco is very relieved his turn is over. Notice how, nervously, he says: Nay, stand and unfold yourself" when Bernardo calls to him. He is, he says, ". . . sick at heart"—presumably with fear lest the "thing" should appear again. This short opening contains very few words, but we can guess from them all we need to know about the situation. Horatio does not believe in their ghost: "Tush, 'twill not appear" he says; and we can picture Bernardo telling his tale, with Marcellus keen to see that he makes no mistake, and Horatio not really paying much attention.

When the Ghost has made its first appearance, and the men

are wondering whether this is an ill omen, Horatio recalls another
famous supernatural event:

> In the most high and palmy state of Rome,
> A little ere the mightiest Julius fell,
> The graves stood tenantless, and the sheeted dead
> Did squeak and gibber in the Roman streets . . .

The crowing of the cock—a simple device—serves two purposes:
it sends the Ghost away; and it is the signal for the guard to
disperse, now that night is over. They go to tell Hamlet what
they have seen; mention of Hamlet leads neatly on to the next
scene, in which Hamlet appears.

ACT I, SCENE 2: *A state room in the castle. The King is holding a
court. He first thanks his courtiers for their loyal support of himself, and in
particular his decision to marry Gertrude, widow of the late king, Hamlet's
father. He then speaks of the trouble with Norway, and sends two
ambassadors to the uncle of Fortinbras, in hopes to settle the affair
peacefully. He then grants permission to Laertes, son of Polonius, the
Lord Chamberlain, to return to France. He turns next to Hamlet, pleading
with him to cease mourning his dead father; and, in particular, to stay in
Denmark, and not return to Wittenburg to study. Gertrude adds her weight
to this, and Hamlet agrees to stay. When he is left alone, Hamlet broods
upon the marriage of his uncle, King Claudius, to his mother. He clearly
detests Claudius, but is powerless to do anything about it. Now Horatio
appears, accompanied by Marcellus, and they tell Hamlet about the Ghost.
He is very excited, and promises to come that same night to see for
himself.*

The most important information to the audience in this scene
is undoubtedly the references to the death of the king, and the
marriage of his widow, Gertrude, to the present king, Claudius.
Claudius himself hints that it was rather a sudden affair:

> Therefore our sometime sister, now our Queen,
> Th' imperial jointress of this warlike State,
> Have we, as 'twere with a defeated joy,
> With one auspicious and one dropping eye,
> With mirth in funeral and with dirge in marriage,
> In equal scale weighing delight and dole—
> Taken to wife . . .

Hamlet himself, when he is alone, puts it much more strongly:

6

> ... within a month;
> Ere yet the salt of most unrighteous tears
> Had left the flushing in her galled eyes,
> She married ...

When he meets Horatio, he is still smarting about it, and he manages to make a cynical joke of the matter. He asks Horatio why he has come to Denmark:

HORATIO: My lord, I came to see your father's funeral.
HAMLET: I pray thee, do not mock me, fellow-student;
I think it was to see my mother's wedding.
HORATIO: Indeed, my lord, it follow'd hard upon.
HAMLET: Thrift, thrift, Horatio! the funeral baked meats
Did coldly furnish forth the marriage tables.

When he hears that the Ghost has appeared, his first thought is that it is a warning. "I doubt some foul play" he says. He is very excited, restless, and impatient for the night to come, and to show this, the lines are short and sharp, and full of questions.

This scene also contains the first of Hamlet's "soliloquies", beginning with the words: "O, that this too, too solid flesh would melt ..." He is, at first, so weary of life that he appears to be thinking about committing suicide; but, in a moment, he is brooding upon his uncle's remarriage, and the speech becomes an outburst of anger at the thought that his mother should lower herself to marry such a man as Claudius—and so soon after her husband's death.

ACT I, SCENE 3: *Laertes, having got permission to leave for France, is saying farewell to his sister, Ophelia. Like a big brother, he is warning her not to take too seriously Hamlet's offers of love for her. The prince, after all, is heir to the throne, and cannot marry as he chooses; he knows this, and is probably merely amusing himself with her. Polonius appears, and gives his son some good advice for his journey. Then, as Laertes goes, Polonius reiterates his son's warning to Ophelia about Hamlet.*

These three characters are very important to the story. Polonius and his son we have already met, briefly, in the previous scene; now we see the family together. We see how effective it is in Shakespeare to have the scenes following without a break, for here is an affectionate group, a brother and sister very fond of each other, and a father concerned for the welfare of both of them. They are a big contrast to Hamlet, his new "father" and his mother. But the scene is not put there just as a contrast. Polonius appears to be a fussy, long-winded old man, fond of saying everything three times over; Ophelia is gentle, and obedient, and clearly she intends to put her father's advice into practice. What is Hamlet going to think? He has just had one shock (the news of his father's ghost), and he is soon to have another.

ACT I, SCENE 4: *On the battlements. Hamlet is with the guards, waiting for the ghost to appear. As they wait, there rises from the castle below the sound of revelry. Hamlet explains that this is the King, holding a noisy drinking party, and he is going on to say how much this sort of thing harms the reputation of the country when he is interrupted by the appearance of the Ghost. It beckons him away; and, shaking off the restraining hands of his friends, he follows it (Scene 5). The Ghost then tells him that he must revenge the foul murder of the king. It describes how Claudius poured poison into the ear of the sleeping king, sending him to his death without the chance to confess his sins. The Ghost fades, and Horatio and the soldiers catch up with Hamlet. He refuses to tell them what the Ghost said to him; in fact, he speaks so strangely that they suspect that the shock has affected his brain. However, he makes them swear that they will tell nobody what they have seen; and he warns them to take no notice if he should appear to talk in a mad fashion in future.*

These two scenes, which are continuous, contain many important things. First of all, notice how typical of the talkative Hamlet the opening of the scene is. He is eagerly awaiting the Ghost, but he gets so carried away by his remarks about the drinking party that he forgets for the moment what he has come for. In fact, he is talking away when the Ghost appears and interrupts him. When the Ghost tells him the story, we realise that he had already suspected it:

GHOST: . . . but know, thou noble youth,
             The serpent that did sting thy father's life
             Now wears his crown.
HAMLET: O, my prophetic soul!
             My uncle!

We have seen, in the earlier scene, how sweet and reasonable Claudius was, and how apparently sincere and honest he is.

Hamlet, who hated him before, knows no limit to his disgust now:

> O, most pernicious woman!
> O villain, villain, smiling, damned villain!
> My tables; meet it is I set it down
> That one may smile, and smile, and be a villain . . .

He is wildly excited when the soldiers first return, but little by little he becomes calmer. This scene is brilliantly written: we watch the mystification of the soldiers at Hamlet's crazy speech; then—perhaps to humour him—they agree to swear, not once but several times, that they will keep the secret; but by the end of the scene he is sufficiently recovered to warn them, quite rationally, that if he appears to put on an "antic disposition" they are to ignore it.

ACT II, SCENE 1: *Polonius is sending a messenger, Reynaldo, to Laertes (who, you will remember, is in Paris). In addition to taking money and letters, Reynaldo is to make some discreet inquiries about how Laertes is behaving. As Reynaldo goes, Ophelia enters, very distressed. Hamlet has just been to see her, but was so strange in his manner and wild in his appearance that she was afraid he was demented. She has done nothing to offend him, except to return his letters, and refuse to see him; but Polonius now assumes that he is desperately in love with her, and urges her to go with him to tell Claudius of the matter.*

This scene, and the next, show how neatly Shakespeare suggests the passing of time. Laertes has obviously been away for some weeks, or else his father would not already be sending to find out about his behaviour. The scene also shows us what an interfering busybody Polonius is: here we see him spying upon his own son, and now he is preparing to bring the affair of Ophelia and Hamlet before the king. Mention of the king, as so often in Shakespeare, leads to a scene in which the king appears.

In fact, the scenes in this play link up very closely. We had Hamlet threatening to put on an "antic disposition"; now, in the very next scene, we hear this from Ophelia:

> My lord, as I was sewing in my chamber,
> Lord Hamlet, with his doublet all unbraced,
> No hat upon his head; his stockings foul'd,
> Ungarter'd, and down-gyved to his ankle;

Pale as his shirt; his knees knocking each other;
And with a look so piteous in purport
As if he had been loosed out of Hell
To speak of horrors—he comes before me.

Polonius, quite convinced beforehand that Hamlet was not serious, is now equally convinced that he is. He can hardly wait to tell the King his views.

ACT II, SCENE 2: *The King and Queen are welcoming to the court Rosencrantz and Guildenstern, friends of Hamlet's student days. They have been sent for to cheer Hamlet up, to try to shake him out of his melancholy humour. As they go, Polonius enters with the ambassadors, just returned from Norway. They have been successful in persuading the Norwegians to drop the campaign against Denmark. Young Fortinbras now intends to march upon Poland, and asks permission to cross Danish territory with his troops. Polonius next introduces the matter of Hamlet's love for Ophelia. As evidence, he has a love-letter written by Hamlet to her, and he proposes that Claudius and himself should hide behind an arras to hear what the prince will say to her. The King and Queen go, and Polonius tries to engage Hamlet in conversation, but Hamlet merely mocks him. Hamlet then greets his old friends, Rosencrantz and Guildenstern, but he quickly guesses that they have been sent for. He explains to them that it is because he has recently been out of humour that the King has taken the trouble to send for them. Now a company of travelling actors approaches the court, and Hamlet—who recognises most of them as old friends—greets them warmly. He asks the leading actor to speak a speech for him; then he requests for the evening's entertainment a piece called "the murder of Gonzago"—with the addition of a few lines written by Hamlet himself. Finally, left alone, Hamlet asks himself how it is that this leading actor appears to be more concerned over the death of a character in a play than he, Hamlet, is over the murder of his own father. He curses his own lack of resolution; and then resolves to use the play to be performed that evening as a device to trap his guilty uncle.*

At the beginning of this very long scene we have, first of all, another example of time passing. Rosencrantz and Guildenstern have been sent for, and have now arrived; the ambassadors, sent out in Act I, Scene 2, have had time to reach Norway and return again to Elsinore.

Several interesting points of character emerge here. Claudius and Gertrude seem genuinely concerned at Hamlet's behaviour: the Queen says:

> Thanks, Guildenstern and gentle Rosencrantz
> And I beseech you instantly to visit
> My too-much-changed son . . .

When Polonius suggests that he has found the reason for Hamlet's "lunacy", the King exclaims at once: "Oh, speak of that; that do I long to hear." But it is Polonius who reveals himself most in this scene. We have already found him long-winded, and interfering; here he is again, and so tedious is his rambling introduction that Gertrude tells him to waste less time, and get to the point. Then his proposal, that they should spy on Hamlet from behind an arras, is typical of his crafty ways (later on, it is to prove his downfall). It is, perhaps, a little cruel of Hamlet to torment the old man, especially since his age is the one thing he can do nothing about, but the audience has already decided that Polonius is not just an old fool, but a rather dangerous one, and so in the little "mad" scene with Hamlet their sympathies will almost certainly be with the prince. This is an effective scene on the stage, with Hamlet pretending to read, and anxious to keep himself to himself; Polonius, determined to talk to Hamlet, and getting nothing but insults for his pains.

As Rosencrantz and Guildenstern enter, the mood changes completely. The three men laugh and joke together, until Hamlet confesses that he has lost all pleasure in life: ". . . man delights not me: no, nor woman neither, though by your smiling you seem to say so." It is, after all, natural that when a young, rich and healthy man is melancholy, his friends might assume that he is in love.

(We come now to a very difficult few lines, which are often cut in performance. It appears that, toward the end of Elizabeth's reign, several companies of boy actors were gaining popularity, and this was much resented by the established players. Hamlet, Rosencrantz and Guildenstern talk in an amusing manner about this recent development. Most of the point of the lines is now lost, and although the passage does help to introduce the players who are approaching the court, it can with profit be left out altogether.)

The scene with the players shows Hamlet at his most gay and charming. He remembers them all, and is delighted to see them; he notices that one of the men now has a beard, another—who sometimes plays women's parts—is much taller than he was, and so on. He asks for a speech, and he gets a fiery and emotional performance.

The scene ends with another "soliloquy"—and it sounds very much as if Hamlet is angry with himself for not having revenged his dead father before this:

> . . . for it cannot be
> That I am pigeon-liver'd, and lack gall
> To make oppression bitter; or, ere this,
> I should have fatted all the region kites
> With this slave's offal. Bloody, bawdy villain!
> Remorseless, treacherous, lecherous, kindless villain!
> O, vengeance!

He then reproaches himself for cursing, and decides that the performance of the play will help to resolve his doubts:

> The spirit that I have seen
> May be the Devil; and the Devil hath power
> T'assume a pleasing shape; yea, and perhaps,
> Out of my weakness and my melancholy,
> As he is very potent with such spirits,
> Abuses me to damn me. I'll have grounds
> More relative than this: the play's the thing
> Wherein I'll catch the conscience of the King.

You will notice a very interesting thing about the play. Here we are, already more than one-third through the play, and every scene has brought us something new and something interesting; yet Hamlet has done nothing about his father's murder. He has talked a good deal, sometimes sensibly, sometimes not, and sometimes to himself, but he has done nothing. Perhaps there is no hurry, and he is right to "make sure" before taking the fatal step; but is he *really* making sure, or is he just putting off the moment of action? He was sure enough, when he met the Ghost, that it was genuine. Do we begin to suspect that Hamlet is *not* a man of action, that he is not really able to bring himself to kill Claudius? Well, if Hamlet is going to delay and delay, something will have to happen to bring the play's action to a climax.

Mention of the King, in the last line of this scene, leads us naturally to a scene in which the King appears. We are by now expecting that Polonius will have made arrangements to spy on Hamlet and Ophelia—as, indeed, he has.

ACT III, SCENE 1: *Rosencrantz and Guildenstern report to the King on their meeting with Hamlet, and at the same time invite the King to attend the play which the players are preparing. Polonius places Ophelia, with a book in her hand, where Hamlet will encounter her, while he and the King hide nearby. Hamlet comes, talking to himself; then, seeing Ophelia, he speaks to her. At first he is polite; but soon he grows enraged, and suggests that, as she is beautiful, she should shut herself away before she becomes evil and corrupt. His violent words leave her distressed, and desperately sorry for him. Claudius, having overheard, concludes that Hamlet is not suffering the anguish of love, nor is he mad; nevertheless, it would be a convenience if he left the court for a time, perhaps as ambassador to England, which owes money to the Danish crown.*

Claudius comes into more prominence with this scene. He is at first delighted that Hamlet is interested in the players, and he urges Rosencrantz and Guildenstern to encourage Hamlet in such pleasures. However, a little later, when he has heard the talk with Ophelia, Claudius is seriously worried:

POLONIUS: . . . My lord, do as you please;
            But, if you hold it fit, after the play
            Let his Queen mother all alone entreat him
            To show his grief: let her be round with him;
            And I'll be placed, so please you, in the ear
            Of all their conference. If she find him not,
            To England send him: or confine him where
            Your wisdom best shall think.
CLAUDIUS: It shall be so;
            Madness in great ones must not unwatch'd go.

Things are, indeed, beginning to happen. Once more we find the busybody, Polonius, suggesting that he be appointed to spy upon Hamlet's private conversation. Once again, as he has done several times in the play, Shakespeare gives us something to look forward to.

The scene with Ophelia begins with yet another "soliloquy"— this time the most famous one of all. Hamlet is once again thinking about ending his life; but this time, unlike his previous

outburst against his mother's remarriage, he is very calm, trying
to reason out the pros and cons of death. If death were the end of
a tedious life, all would be well; but who knows what comes *after*
death, for who has ever returned to this life to tell the tale?
Strangely enough, toward the end of this speech Hamlet seems
to be hinting at the reason for his unwillingness to act on his
ghostly father's instructions:

> Thus conscience does make cowards of us all;
> And thus the native hue of resolution
> Is sicklied o'er with the pale cast of thought,
> And enterprises of great pith and moment,
> With this regard, their currents turn awry,
> And lose the name of action—

In talking to Ophelia, Hamlet seems to be back in the mood of an
earlier speech, when he exclaimed against his mother's remarriage
with the words: "Frailty, thy name is woman!" He seems now
to assume that all women are alike; in fact, he seems to have
forgotten that he is talking to Ophelia:

> I have heard of your paintings, too, well enough; God has given you
> one face, and you make yourselves another; you jig, you amble, and you
> lisp, and nickname God's creatures, and make your wantonness your
> ignorance. Go to, I'll no more on't; it hath made me mad. I say, we will
> have no more marriages; those that are married already all but one, shall
> live; the rest shall keep as they are. To a nunnery, go!

ACT III, SCENE 2: *The play is about to begin, and Hamlet, in a lively
mood again, is giving the actors good advice about the performance. Then
Horatio enters. Hamlet first sings his praises as a true and loyal friend,
then tells him of the play and its special meaning. Horatio promises to
watch the King closely during the performance. The court assembles, and
Hamlet sits by Ophelia, with whom he jokes until the play begins. The
performers first present a dumb-show, and then the play itself follows.
The language is flowery and rather a bore, but the action is swift and
obvious. As the play nears its end, Hamlet, suddenly excited, leaps up to
add his commentary. The King rises, calls for light, and goes abruptly
out. Hamlet is crowing to Horatio at his success, when the message comes
that his mother wishes to speak to him. Before he goes, he has a brief scene
with Rosencrantz and Guildenstern in which he attacks them for trying to
deceive him with false friendship.*

This is a splendid scene to act, full of movement and contrast. It begins with an excited Hamlet, telling his friends the players how to act the scene. This helps to prepare the ground for the performance; but it is also very important dramatically, for there will be no point in Hamlet's scheme to expose Claudius if the play is not understood. When the court enters, with a great show of ceremony, Hamlet suddenly starts to act his "madness"—and here the reactions of the other characters are very important. We can picture the sudden silence, and the buzz of conversation, when Hamlet refuses to sit by his mother:

GERTRUDE: Come hither, my dear Hamlet, sit by me.
HAMLET: No, good mother: Here's metal more attractive. (*To Ophelia*)
POLONIUS: O ho! Do you mark that? (*Aside to the king*)

Hamlet's talk to Ophelia must cause some embarrassment to those present; either that, or we must imagine that the rest are so busy gossiping that they do not hear it, for Hamlet is extraordinarily coarse to Ophelia: he makes bawdy jokes, and treats her without any dignity or respect. But he also says something which is, once again, a clue to his anger:

HAMLET: . . . What should a man do but be merry? for, look you, how cheerfully my mother looks, and my father died within these two hours.
OPHELIA: Nay, 'tis twice two months, my lord.
HAMLET: So long? . . .

The play begins with a dumb-show—in other words, the plot is enacted briefly without words, and then again, in much more detail, with the dialogue. The play wounds the conscience of Claudius so much that he leaves the room; perhaps you are wondering why the dumb-show does not have the same effect upon him. This is the sort of problem which performers have to settle for themselves, but the most likely explanation is that he was not watching it. Many plays in Elizabethan times had this kind of introduction; and, since it added nothing to the meaning, it might well have been ignored. Hamlet's excitement when his ruse works is boundless; he breaks into rhyme, childishly, and we can picture him almost dancing with joy. But now come Rosencrantz and Guildenstern; and now we see why Hamlet spoke that

touching speech to his loyal friend, Horatio. It was to show up
the false friends whom he now turns upon. He is bitterly angry—
spoiling for a fight, you may say; he grabs a recorder from one of
the actors, forces it into Guildenstern's hands, and commands
him to play it. Guildenstern, who is no musician, protests his
inability:

HAMLET: . . . Look you, these are the stops.
GUILDENSTERN: But these cannot I command to any utterance of harmony,
                I have not the skill.
HAMLET: Why, look you now, how unworthy a thing you make of
                me! You would play upon me; you would seem to know
                my stops; you would pluck out the heart of my mystery;
                you would sound me from my lowest note to the top of my
                compass; and there is much music, excellent voice, in this
                little organ; yet cannot you make it speak. 'Sblood, do
                you think I am easier to be played on than a pipe? . . .

Hamlet is summoned again to his mother. As he turns to go, we
hear a few lines which remind us of *Macbeth,* with its constant
references to evil and to darkness. They help to reflect the mood
of Hamlet, and to remind us that it is his mother's marriage to his
uncle which lies at the back of all his morbid thoughts:

'Tis now the very witching time of night,
When churchyards yawn, and Hell itself breathes out
Contagion to this world: now could I drink hot blood,
And do such bitter business as the day
Would quake to look on . . .

ACT III, SCENE 3: *Claudius, conferring with Rosencrantz and Guildenstern, has definitely decided to send Hamlet to England, escorted by these
two. They go to prepare for the journey; Polonius tells the King that he
intends to hide in the Queen's room to hear Hamlet speak with her; and
then Claudius is left alone. He has been severely shaken by the play, and
is now, full of remorse, trying to pray for some kind of relief. As he kneels,
Hamlet enters, and for a moment contemplates killing Claudius there and
then. Then he recalls how Claudius killed his father without any confession
of sins, and he resolves to perform the act when Claudius, likewise, is
unprepared.*

It is interesting how, in this short scene, Claudius has reached
the end of his patience with Hamlet, and has resolved to pack

him off to England. Hamlet has a chance, here, to strike the blow, but decides against it, and we cannot help wondering whether he will delay and delay until it is too late. The scene ends as he goes to his mother's room—where the next scene takes place.

ACT III, SCENE 4: *Polonius hides again behind an arras, and Hamlet enters his mother's room. His manner so frightens her that she cries out, afraid he might injure her. Polonius calls for help, and Hamlet, quickly drawing his sword, runs the old man through. Hamlet then confronts his mother with her crime: she has married a murderer—and, what is more, a man who was not worth a straw compared with her dead husband. The Queen is appalled at all he is saying, but he is interrupted by the Ghost, who has come to remind him of his still unfinished task. Gertrude, who can neither see nor hear the Ghost, assumes that Hamlet is raving. With his last words, he tells her he is to go to England, and he seems to be fore-warned of a plot against him. He goes out, dragging the dead Polonius after him.*

This is, perhaps, the most important scene in the play. Notice how Shakespeare has kept us waiting for this private meeting; and notice how many things follow from this short but vital scene. Firstly, Polonius is killed, and at last Claudius has tangible evidence of Hamlet's violence; but we have to wait a little longer before we see the effect of Polonius's death on Ophelia, his daugher, and Laerteş, his son. Then the appearance of the Ghost, which seems to be telling Hamlet that, if he does not act quickly, it will be too late:

> "Do not forget: this visitation
> Is but to whet thy almost blunted purpose."

The Ghost's concern for Gertrude, and her obvious distress, suggest that she was not aware that Claudius was the killer of her husband. Together they seem to be telling him to concentrate on the murderer, instead—as he has been—of brooding on his mother's wickedness.

We have seen many times already how changeable Hamlet's moods can be. He is gay and charming one minute, savage and cynical the next, and even in this scene he is something of a contradiction. After the Ghost has warned him to be gentle with his mother, he pleads with her not to consort with Claudius:

GEETRUDE: O Hamlet, thou has cleft my heart in twain.
HAMLET: O throw away the worser part of it,
And live the purer with the other half.
Good night: but go not to my uncle's bed;
Assume a virtue if you have it not . . .

Then, speaking of Polonius, he says:

"For this same lord
I do repent . . .
I will bestow him, and will answer well
The death I gave him. So, again, good night . . .

He then speaks a rhymed couplet (the customary way to end a scene in Shakespeare)—and we might expect this to be the end of the scene. But Hamlet suddenly repeats, in much coarser language, what he has just said: "my uncle" becomes "the bloat King"—with a good deal of unpleasant detail omitted the first time. When he gets to Polonius, he is similarly coarse:

This man shall set me packing:
I'll lug the guts into the neighbour room.
Mother, good night . . .

Another rhymed couplet, and the scene finally closes.

Is this evidence that two versions of the play have somehow got mixed together? Or is it just the playwright's way of showing us a changeable Hamlet, gentle one moment, violent the next? The producer must decide; and, having decided, he will shorten the scene—or not—as he thinks best.

The death of Polonius may have been an accident, but it has far-reaching consequences. After this very emotional scene between Hamlet and his mother, Shakespeare gives us three quite short scenes, full of movement and panic, to show the upheaval caused by Hamlet's action.

ACT III, SCENE 5: *Gertrude tells Claudius that Hamlet has killed Polonius. She believes him to be mad. Claudius, realising that he himself might have been the victim, sends Rosencrantz and Guildenstern to find Hamlet, and to carry the body into the chapel.*

Gertrude, having heard Hamlet speak to the (apparently non-existent) Ghost, assumes her son to be out of his mind. Claudius, however, sees the danger in his continuing at large:

O heavy deed!
It had been so with us, had we been there:
His liberty is full of threats to all . . .

It looks as if the death of Polonius will make Hamlet's revenge even more difficult to accomplish.

ACT III, SCENE 6: *A very short scene. Hamlet has hidden the body, and now Rosencrantz and Guildenstern come to bring him to the King. He stalls them for a moment, and then runs off, the other two in pursuit.*

The Elizabethan stage was perfect for this kind of scene. Hamlet is chased by Rosencrantz and Guildenstern (assisted, no doubt, by the King's servants), and the open platform stage, with its several entrances, lends itself very well to the swift movement called for.

ACT III, SCENE 7: *Hamlet is caught, and brought before Claudius. The King informs him that he is to go to England; and, when he is alone, Claudius reveals that Hamlet is to die as a result of the plans he has made.*

We are seeing more and more of Claudius's determination to deal with Hamlet. He begins the scene with a speech expressing his intention to handle the matter firmly but tactfully; he ends the scene with the decision to have Hamlet killed.

Between the two speeches, we see in Hamlet the same wild, jesting mood that he was in during the "play" scene. His hatred of Claudius is open now, and his lack of regard for his own safety comes out in the insolence of his replies:

CLAUDIUS: Where is Polonius?
HAMLET: In Heaven; send thither to see; if your messenger find him not
           there, seek him in the other place yourself. But indeed, if
           you find him not within this month, you may nose him as you
           go up the stairs into the lobby.
CLAUDIUS: Go seek him there (*to some attendants*).
HAMLET: He will stay till you come.

ACT IV, SCENE 1: *You will remember that Claudius gave permission for a Norwegian army to cross his territory. Now Hamlet, on his way to take ship for England, meets a Captain and a party of soldiers. He asks what the campaign is about, and is told that they are waging war for a small piece of land that is not worth bothering about. Hamlet, left to himself, wonders how it is that men can fight so bravely for a futile cause, while he seems unable to take action over his own father's murder.*

The scene serves two purposes: it shows us Hamlet's departure from Denmark; and it once again (as did the "play" scene) gives Hamlet the opportunity to realise how much time he has wasted:

> How all occasions do inform against me
> And spur my dull revenge!

He tries, once more, to stir himself up to take decisive action:

>   . . . O, from this time forth,
> My thoughts be bloody, or be nothing worth!

ACT IV, SCENE 2: *Horatio brings word to the Queen that Ophelia is mad; a few moments later she comes in, singing old songs, and talking wildly. Claudius is in time to hear part of her wanderings, and he realises that her father's death is probably the cause. Claudius is seriously worried; so many things have gone wrong, and the hushed-up burial of Polonius will not satisfy Laertes, who has returned from France. At this point Laertes, backed by armed men, bursts in, demanding revenge for the murder of his father. Claudius is reasoning with him, when Ophelia returns, and Laertes sees her mad condition. As she goes out, Claudius promises Laertes that he shall have a full explanation of all that has happened.*

Ophelia's madness at her father's death is quite different from Hamlet's wild behaviour. She sings, talks prettily, and hands out imaginary flowers to Gertrude, Claudius, and Laertes. Her madness is pathetic, because she is quite innocent of any crime, and the scene is obviously intended to move us to pity for her.

The most important thing in this scene is the appearance of Laertes. He, like Hamlet, has a father's death to revenge; but what a difference there is in the two men! Laertes is ready to murder there and then, if need be, and he will not be put off with false answers. Gertrude, afraid for Claudius's life, tries to hold Laertes back, but Claudius stands bravely up to him:

CLAUDIUS: . . . Tell me, Laertes,
                Why thou are thus incensed.—Let him go, Gertrude—
                Speak, man.
LAERTES: Where is my father?
CLAUDIUS: Dead.

GERTRUDE: But not by him.
CLAUDIUS: Let him demand his fill.
LAERTES: How came he dead? I'll not be juggled with:
             To Hell, allegiance! Vows, to the blackest devil!
             Conscience and grace, to the profoundest pit!
             I dare damnation: to this point I stand,
             That both the worlds I give to negligence,
             Let come what comes; only I'll be revenged
             Most throughly for my father.

Compare this with Hamlet's indecision, and you can see that, once Laertes hears who murdered his father, there is little doubt which way the game will go. But Hamlet has been sent to England, and to his death—or so we think. The next scene, which is very short, sets the scene for the conflict between Hamlet and Laertes.

ACT IV, SCENE 3: *Sailors bring letters for Horatio; one for himself, from Hamlet, the others for the King. It appears that Hamlet was captured by a pirate vessel, and has now been landed in Denmark. He seeks a meeting with Horatio.*

This scene is very neatly placed. At the end of the previous scene, we have Claudius offering to tell Laertes the full story of his father's death, and now we have the news that Hamlet is back in Denmark. You can see how the two men are drawing more closely together.

ACT IV, SCENE 4: *Claudius has told Laertes how Hamlet plotted against his life, and how he murdered Polonius. Laertes wants to know why the King allowed him to stay unpunished, but Claudius explains how fond Gertrude is of her son, and how popular Hamlet is with the people of Denmark. At this point a letter reaches the King from Hamlet, giving the news of his return. The King's plot to have Hamlet killed has obviously miscarried; he now proposes that Laertes should challenge Hamlet to a friendly fencing-match. One sword without a guard on it—aided by a little poison on the tip—and Hamlet should not survive the duel. Gertrude now enters, with the news that Ophelia, heedlessly gathering flowers by a stream, fell into it and was drowned.*

Here we see again how different Laertes is from Hamlet. Claudius himself puts his finger on it when he says that the longer we delay an act of this kind, the less likely we are to do it at all. He might be describing Hamlet's failure in these words:

CLAUDIUS: . . . That we would do,
          We should do when we would; for this *would* changes,
          And hath abatements and delays as many
          As there are tongues, are hands, are accidents . . .
          . . . Hamlet comes back: what would you undertake
          To show yourself your father's son in deed
          More than in words?
LAERTES: To cut his throat in the church.
CLAUDIUS: No place indeed should murder sanctuarize;
          Revenge should have no bounds.

The beautiful description of Ophelia's death leads on to the next scene, which is a graveyard. It also helps to keep Laertes's anger on the boil.

Act V, SCENE 1: *Two gravediggers are arguing about whether a suicide should be given a Christian burial. There seems to be some doubt about the death of the person whose grave this is to be, and we can guess from their remarks that it is Ophelia. Hamlet and Horatio enter; Hamlet talks with the gravedigger; and, though he jokes with him, Hamlet's thoughts are very much on the subject of death. As they talk, a funeral procession approaches, and the body of Ophelia, attended by Gertrude, Claudius and Laertes, is carried in. As Hamlet and Horatio stand to one side, the body is laid in the grave, and Laertes, overcome with grief, leaps into the grave; at which point Hamlet does the same, and the two men struggle together until they are separated.*

This is, in a way, the most comic and the most serious scene in the play. The First Gravedigger is something of a wit, and Hamlet takes pleasure in bandying words with him. The gravedigger, having done this job so often, is no longer overawed by it; but to Hamlet there is something terrifying in the thought of death. His question: "How long will a man lie in the earth ere he rot?" has a morbid edge to it. Then, when the gravedigger hands him the skull of Yorick, the old king's jester, Hamlet thinks more seriously of the matter; and then, as so often in this play, his thoughts turn to his disgust with women:

> . . . Where be your gibes now, your gambols, your songs, your flashes of merriment, that were wont to set the table in a roar? Not one now, to mock your own grinning? quite chop-fallen? Now get you to my lady's chamber, and tell her, let her paint an inch thick, to this favour she will come: make her laugh at that!

It is now that the procession enters. Laertes is distressed that no proper ceremonials accompany the burial; then, as Gertrude strews flowers on the corpse, Hamlet realises who the dead one is. He steps forward, to challenge Laertes with the words: "It is I, Hamlet the Dane." This is a tremendous moment in the play, for we know that Claudius is already arranging a fatal duel between these two men. Now they fight for a moment over the body of Ophelia—her brother, and the man who was in love with her.

However, Hamlet's ravings at the graveside are taken for madness by most of those present, who know how madly he has behaved lately. Horatio goes after him, to calm him down; Laertes goes with Claudius, to perfect their plan of revenge.

ACT V, SCENE 2: *The final scene. Hamlet is explaining to Horatio all that has happened since his departure for England. He tells him that, during the pirate attack, he opened the documents carried by Rosencrantz and Guildenstern, and there discovered instructions for his own execution when he reached England. He therefore altered the documents to include their names instead of his own. Now, having discovered proof of Claudius's treachery, he is quite ready to kill him. He is expressing his regret at having quarrelled with Laertes, whom he likes, when a messenger brings a challenge to fight a duel before the King. Hamlet agrees, and the audience assemble. In addition to the poisoned sword, the King has prepared a cup of poisoned wine, which he places alongside his own goblet. Hamlet is winning, and the King ostentatiously drinks his health; but, before Claudius can stop her, Gertrude seizes the poisoned cup and drinks from it. Laertes wounds Hamlet, who, changing swords with him, wounds him in turn. As he falls dying, Laertes confesses his treachery, and that of the King, whereupon Hamlet turns the poisoned weapon upon his uncle. Hamlet dies as the march of soldiers is heard in the distance. Fortinbras, returning from Poland, and the ambassadors returned from England, enter the scene. Horatio declares his intention of making the whole tragic story known to the people, and Fortinbras arranges for the disposal of the bodies.*

This final scene has three sections, each one carefully built up to create the maximum dramatic effect. First of all, after the unseemly struggles by the graveside, we have a quiet passage in which Hamlet describes his dealings with the documents. It ends, ironically, as he expresses his regret at having offended Laertes, little knowing that it is this same Laertes who is plotting to kill him.

... But I am very sorry, good Horatio,
That to Laertes I forgot myself;
For by the image of my cause I see
The portraiture of his ...

These last two lines are particularly striking, because Hamlet is saying that Laertes, like himself, has a father's death to avenge.

Mention of Laertes brings in the next part of the scene, as Osric, the young courtier, brings the challenge to the duel. Osric is a dandified, affected young man, and Hamlet takes an instant dislike to his curious manners, so he decides, by speaking to him in an even more ludicrous way, to make a fool of him. This comic interlude is but the calm before the wreck, and Hamlet hints to Horatio that he has an uneasy feeling that something serious is going to happen. But he will not postpone the duel; he is not so fond of living—as we know—to care very much whether he dies or not:

... If it be now, 'tis not to come; if it be not to come, it will
be now; if it be not now, then it will come; the readiness is all. ...

And so we move into the last scene. It seems all the more tragic that Hamlet's only thought, before this duel begins, is to win forgiveness from Laertes, and he speaks to him in gentle and dignified language:

His madness is poor Hamlet's enemy.
Sir, in this audience,
Let my disclaiming from a purposed evil
Free me so far in your most generous thoughts,
That I have shot mine arrow o'er the house,
And hurt my brother.

Then comes the fight. Notice how, when they have chosen their weapons, Laertes finds fault with his, so that he can pick up the poisoned foil instead. Notice, too, that Hamlet is probably touched by a foul blow—that is, a blow struck before he is ready, since Laertes so far has failed to strike him at all. Then comes a sudden change: till now Hamlet has been merely playing, but now, feeling the prick of the blade, he seizes Laertes's weapon, forces him to exchange, and gives a fatal blow in his turn. The "fortunate coincidence" of Fortinbras's return to Denmark enables the bodies to be borne from the stage; but it also ensures that, accompanied by the slow drum-beats of the soldiers, the final procession of corpses will have a powerful dignity.

So Hamlet has at last won his revenge; but it is not the calculated revenge which the Ghost urged upon him. Compared with the cunning of Claudius, the swift action of Laertes, Hamlet is more a thinker than a doer, and the play ends as it does, not because Hamlet had planned it all, but because—after the accidental death of Polonius—the intrigues and the plots caught up with Hamlet, and swept him along with them.

Words and deeds

Hamlet is a play full of action, and one remarkable thing about the play is the great variety of movement from one scene to another. Compare, for instance, the two "battlement" scenes: notice, in the first one, how the short lines suggest nervousness, even dread, of the Ghost; the guards are "jumpy"—and, to make it more stark, Shakespeare stresses the coldness of the night. Notice with what relief the soldiers welcome the daylight, which means that they can go off duty for a while. Anyone acting this scene has no difficulty in imagining the situation. The second time, however, things are different. Now the soldiers are not so much afraid as excited and curious. Hamlet is talking about Claudius, but the soldiers are only half-listening; it is they, and not Hamlet, who see the Ghost first. Then there is the struggle to prevent Hamlet from doing himself some injury; finally, after the Ghost has been and gone, comes the half-mad scene in which the soldiers, quite bewildered by Hamlet's words, are made to swear upon his sword.

The scenes of pomp and ceremony are similarly contrasted. In the first one, the court is assembled to conduct affairs of state; the ambassadors bow themselves out, Laertes kneels to beg a favour of the King, the courtiers group themselves respectfully round the room—only Hamlet sits apart, silent and sullen. We hear his sulky replies to the King's kindly speeches, and his grudging acceptance of his mother's request. At the "play" scene, however, things are very different. The court assembles in ones and twos, with a murmur of conversation about the play they are going to see; Claudius, during the dumb-show, drinks, or talks to

Gertrude, or jokes with one of the courtiers; Hamlet, in spite of his "merry" words to Ophelia, is full of suppressed excitement. As the play reaches its climax, so does the scene: the actors play the murder, Hamlet's voice joins in the action, the King rises and rushes out, and the play breaks off. The last "court" scene is, in fact, the last scene of the play. Here the excitement is really tension, as we wait for the duel to begin. Everyone present knows that Hamlet killed Polonius, Laertes's father; and everyone must be wondering how "friendly" the duel is to be. In deathly quiet the fight begins; then the panic spreads as things begin to go wrong. Gertrude drinks the poison; the two men change weapons; Claudius tries, in vain, to stop the fighting; and then the final blows are struck, and the violence is followed by a quiet, solemn death scene and funeral procession.

Quite often, too, the action of a single scene is interrupted by a sudden new event which affects the behaviour of the characters. Hamlet, talking to his old friend, Horatio, is suddenly bowled over by the news of the Ghost's appearance. Can you see him, pacing restlessly up and down, darting questions at the other two, so upset and excited that he cannot keep still? Then there is the very tense scene in which Laertes, out for blood, faces Claudius with the threat of death if he does not account for Polonius's murder. The two men confront each other, and Claudius is beginning to reason with Laertes, when the mad Ophelia is suddenly allowed into the room. How does Laertes react to this?

Even the scenes with only one or two characters have their moments of sudden violent action. As Hamlet talks to Gertrude, he handles her so roughly that she cries out for help; then, when Hamlet draws his sword upon the figure behind the arras, her fear becomes a sudden shout of horror at what he is about to do. We get the same shock of surprise when Hamlet, after the quietness of "To be or not to be", suddenly starts to bully Ophelia; or when he steps out of the shadows in the graveyard scene and confronts Laertes across his sister's grave.

A human tragedy

It is the custom, when talking about plays of this kind, to refer to the "tragic hero"—but, if this sounds as if the main character is a great and virtuous man surrounded by villains, it is quite misleading. Hamlet has many fine qualities: he is charming, sensitive, considerate and loyal to his friends, sharply critical of the weaknesses of others; he is, on the other hand, moody and changeable, bitter and cruel to Ophelia, Polonius, and Gertrude, unscrupulous in his dealings with Rosencrantz and Guildenstern. He is a very "human" person, but he is not a model of Christian goodness. "Tragic hero" really means a man of noble birth and honest character, whose downfall is the result of his own weakness as much as the machinations of others. Hamlet postpones revenge, until revenge of another sort catches up with him.

As with the hero, so with the other characters in the play. Claudius has certainly performed a most wicked crime, but he is not out to destroy Hamlet from the beginning. Indeed, until Hamlet's behaviour becomes too dangerous to tolerate, all Claudius wants is for him to live in peace at Elsinore until the time comes for him to take over the throne. Laertes is the virtual slayer of Hamlet, but he, too, is no villain; he is a good man, liked and respected by the people, highly esteemed by Hamlet himself. He is driven to murder by his grief at the deaths of his father and sister, and his rage at the man he believes to have been responsible. Polonius, "tedious old fool" though he may be, acts always from the best of intentions. He dies, mistaken for the King, in an attempt to discover the truth about Hamlet's strange behaviour. Gertrude's great love for her son is constantly referred to in the play, and it seems clear that, until "the closet scene", she had no idea how bitterly Hamlet resents her marriage to Claudius.

What is clear when we read *Hamlet*—and still clearer when we act the play, or see it acted—is that, although none of the characters is "ordinary" or commonplace, each one is a mixture of good and bad qualities such as we see in the people who surround us in real life. This may be, in part, the reason why people return to this play over and over again, because they recognise the truth of the characters, and they realise that, under these circumstances, their behaviour is perfectly convincing.

Finally, the play will always fascinate people because it does not give a clear answer to quite a number of tantalising questions. Hamlet *pretends* to be mad; but just how sane is he? for his conduct is certainly not "normal"—is it? Gertrude is most distressed at Hamlet's attack upon her; but how much did she really know about her first husband's death? Claudius is a clever diplomat, and a smooth and easy talker; but how much of what he says—particularly about his concern for Hamlet—is really sincere?

A large part of the pleasure to be had from *Hamlet* is to see a good performance of it. Part of the fascination of the play is that each performance suggests different answers to these questions.

PERGAMON OXFORD ENGLISH SERIES
General Editor: D. MATTAM

PLAYS IN ACTION